MongoDB Data M

Focus on data usage and better design schemas with the help of MongoDB

Wilson da Rocha França

PUBLISHING

BIRMINGHAM - MUMBAI

MongoDB Data Modeling

First published: June 2015

Production reference: 1160615

Published by Packt Publishing Ltd.
Livery Place
35 Livery Street
Birmingham B3 2PB, UK.

ISBN 978-1-78217-534-6

www.packtpub.com

Credits

Author
Wilson da Rocha França

Reviewers
Mani Bhushan
Álvaro García Gómez
Mohammad Hasan Niroomand
Mithun Satheesh

Commissioning Editor
Dipika Gaonkar

Content Development Editor
Merwyn D'souza

Technical Editors
Dhiraj Chandanshive
Siddhi Rane

Copy Editor
Ameesha Smith-Green

Project Coordinator
Neha Bhatnagar

Proofreader
Safis Editing

Indexer
Priya Sane

Graphics
Sheetal Aute
Disha Haria

Production Coordinator
Shantanu N. Zagade

Cover Work
Shantanu N. Zagade

About the Author

Wilson da Rocha França is a system architect at the leading online retail company in Latin America. An IT professional, passionate about computer science, and an open source enthusiast, he graduated with a university degree from Centro Federal de Educação Tecnológica Celso Suckow da Fonseca, Rio de Janeiro, Brazil, in 2005 and holds a master's degree in Business Administration from Universidade Federal de Rio de Janeiro, gained in 2010.

Passionate about e-commerce and the Web, he has had the opportunity to work not only in online retail but in other markets such as comparison shopping and online classifieds. He has dedicated most of his time to being a Java web developer.

He worked as a reviewer on *Instant Varnish Cache How-to* and *Arduino Development Cookbook*, both by Packt Publishing.

Acknowledgments

I honestly never thought I would write a book so soon in my life. When the *MongoDB Data Modeling* project was presented to me, I embraced this challenge and I have always believed that it was possible to do. However, to be able to start and accomplish this project would not have been possible without the help of the Acquisition Editor, Hemal Desai and the Content Development Editor, Merwyn D'Souza. In addition, I would like to thank the Project Coordinator, Judie Jose, who understood all my delayed deliveries of the *Arduino Development Cookbook* reviews, written in parallel with this book.

Firstly, I would like to mention the Moutinho family, who were very important in the development of this project. Roberto Moutinho, for your support and for opening this door for me. Renata Moutinho, for your patience, friendship, and kindness, from the first to the last chapter; you guided me and developed my writing skills in this universal language that is not my mother tongue. Thank you very much Renata.

I would like to thank my teachers for their unique contributions in my education that improved my knowledge. This book is also for all Brazilians. I am very proud to be born in Brazil.

During the development of this book, I had to distance myself a little bit from my friends and family. Therefore, I want to apologize to everyone.

Mom and Dad, thank you for your support and the opportunities given to me. Your unconditional love made me the man that I am. A man that believes he is able to achieve his objectives in life. Rafaela, Marcelo, Igor, and Natália, you inspire me, make me happy, and make me feel like the luckiest brother on Earth. Lucilla, Maria, Wilson, and Nilton, thanks for this huge and wonderful family. Cado, wherever you are, you are part of this too.

And, of course, I could not forget to thank my wife, Christiane. She supported me during the whole project, and understood every time we stayed at home instead of going out together or when I went to bed too late. She not only proofread but also helped me a lot with the translations of each chapter before I submitted them to Packt Publishing. Chris, thanks for standing beside me. My life began at the moment I met you. I love you.

About the Reviewers

Mani Bhushan is Head of Engineering at Swiggy (`http://www.swiggy.com/`) — India's biggest on-demand logistic platform focused on food.

In the past, he worked for companies such as Amazon, where he was a part of the CBA (Checkout by Amazon) team and flexible payment services team, then he moved to Zynga where he had a lot of fun building games and learning game mechanics. His last stint was at Vizury, where he was leading their RTB (Real-Time Bidding) and DMP (Data Management Platform) groups.

He is a religious coder and he codes every day. His GitHub profile is `https://github.com/mbhushan`. He is an avid learner and has done dozens of courses on MOOC platforms such as Coursera and Udacity in areas such as mathematics, music, algorithms, management, machine learning, data mining, and more. You can visit his LinkedIn profile at `http://in.linkedin.com/in/mbhushan`.

All his free time goes to his kid Shreyansh and his wife Archana.

Álvaro García Gómez is a computer engineer specialized in software engineering. From his early days with computers, he showed a special interest in algorithms and how efficient they are. The reason for this is because he is focused on real-time and high performance algorithms for massive data under cloud environments. Tools such as Cassandra, MongoDB, and other NoSQL engines taught him a lot. Although he is still learning about this kind of computation, he was able to write some articles and papers on the subject.

After several years of research in these areas, he arrived in the world of data mining, as a hobby that became a vocation. Since data mining covers the requirements of efficient and fast algorithms and storage engines in a distributed platform, this is the perfect place for him to research and work.

With the intention of sharing and improving his knowledge, he founded a non-profit organization where beginners have a place to learn and experts can use supercomputers for their research (supercomputers built by themselves).

At the moment, he works as a consultant and architecture analyst for big data applications.

Mohammad Hasan Niroomand graduated from the BSc program of software engineering at K. N. Toosi University. He worked as a frontend developer and UI designer in the Sadiq ICT team for 3 years. Now, he is a backend developer at Etick Pars, using Node.js and MongoDB to develop location-based services. Moreover, he is an MSc student at the Sharif University of Technology in the field of software engineering.

Mithun Satheesh is an open source enthusiast and a full stack web developer from India. He has around 5 years of experience in web development, both in frontend and backend programming. He codes mostly in JavaScript, Ruby, and PHP.

He has written a couple of libraries in Node.js and published them on npm, earning a considerable user base. One of these is called node-rules, a forward chaining rule engine implementation written initially to handle transaction risks on Bookmyshow (http://in.bookmyshow.com/)—one of his former employers. He is a regular on programming sites such as Stack Overflow and loves contributing to the open source world.

Along with programming, he is also interested in experimenting with various cloud hosting solutions. He has a number of his applications listed in the developer spotlight of PaaS providers such as Red Hat's OpenShift.

He tweets at @mithunsatheesh.

I would like to thank my parents for allowing me to live the life that I wanted to live. I am thankful to all my teachers and God for whatever I knowledge I have gained in my life.

www.PacktPub.com

Support files, eBooks, discount offers, and more

For support files and downloads related to your book, please visit www.PacktPub.com.

Did you know that Packt offers eBook versions of every book published, with PDF and ePub files available? You can upgrade to the eBook version at www.PacktPub.com and as a print book customer, you are entitled to a discount on the eBook copy. Get in touch with us at service@packtpub.com for more details.

At www.PacktPub.com, you can also read a collection of free technical articles, sign up for a range of free newsletters and receive exclusive discounts and offers on Packt books and eBooks.

https://www2.packtpub.com/books/subscription/packtlib

Do you need instant solutions to your IT questions? PacktLib is Packt's online digital book library. Here, you can search, access, and read Packt's entire library of books.

Why subscribe?

- Fully searchable across every book published by Packt
- Copy and paste, print, and bookmark content
- On demand and accessible via a web browser

Free access for Packt account holders

If you have an account with Packt at www.PacktPub.com, you can use this to access PacktLib today and view 9 entirely free books. Simply use your login credentials for immediate access.

Table of Contents

Preface

Even today, it is still quite common to say that computer science is a young and new field. However, this statement becomes somewhat contradictory when we observe other fields. Unlike other fields, computer science is a discipline that is continually evolving above the normal speed. I dare say that computer science has now set the path of evolution for other fields such as medicine and engineering. In this context, database systems as an area of the computer science discipline has not only contributed to the growth of other fields, but has also taken advantage itself of the evolution and progress of many areas of technology such as computer networks and computer storage.

Formally, database systems have been an active research topic since the 1960s. Since then, we have gone through a few generations, and big names in the IT industry have emerged and started to dictate the market's tendencies.

In the 2000s, driven by the world's Internet access growth, which created a new network traffic profile with the social web boom, the term NoSQL became common. Considered by many to be a paradoxical and polemic subject, it is seen by some as a new technology generation that has been developed in response to all changes we have experienced in the last decade.

MongoDB is one of these technologies. Born in the early 2000s, it became the most popular NoSQL database in the world. Not only the most popular database in the world, since February 2015, MongoDB became the fourth most popular database system according to the DB-Engines ranking (`http://db-engines.com/en/`), surpassing the well-known PostgreSQL database.

Nevertheless, popularity should not be confused with adoption. Although the DB-Engines ranking shows us that MongoDB is responsible for some traffic on search engines such as Google, has job search activity, and has substantial social media activity, we can not state how many applications are using MongoDB as a data source. Indeed, this is not exclusive to MongoDB, but is true of every NoSQL technology.

The good news is that adopting MongoDB has not been a very tough decision to make. It's open source, so you can download it free of charge from MongoDB Inc. (`https://www.mongodb.com`), where you can find extensive documentation. You also can count on a big and growing community, who, like you, are always looking for new stuff on books, blogs, and forums; sharing knowledge and discoveries; and collaborating to add to the MongoDB evolution.

MongoDB Data Modeling was written with the aim of being another research and reference source for you. In it, we will cover the techniques and patterns used to create scalable data models with MongoDB. We will go through basic database modeling concepts, and provide a general overview focused on modeling in MongoDB. Lastly, you will see a practical step-by-step example of modeling a real-life problem.

Primarily, database administrators with some MongoDB background will take advantage of *MongoDB Data Modeling*. However, everyone from developers to all the curious people that downloaded MongoDB will make good use of it.

This book focuses on the 3.0 version of MongoDB. MongoDB 3.0, which was long awaited by the community, is considered by MongoDB Inc. as its most significant release to date. This is because, in this release, we were introduced to the new and highly flexible storage architecture, WiredTiger. Performance and scalability enhancements intend to strengthen MongoDB's emphasis among database systems technologies, and position it as the standard database for modern applications.

What this book covers

Chapter 1, Introducing Data Modeling, introduces you to basic data modeling concepts and the NoSQL universe.

Chapter 2, Data Modeling with MongoDB, gives you an overview of MongoDB's document-oriented architecture and presents you with the document, its characteristics, and how to build it.

Chapter 3, Querying Documents, guides you through MongoDB APIs to query documents and shows you how the query affects our data modeling process.

Chapter 4, Indexing, explains how you can improve the execution of your queries and consequently change the way we model our data by making use of indexes.

Chapter 5, Optimizing Queries, helps you to use MongoDB's native tools to optimize your queries.

Chapter 6, Managing the Data, focuses on the maintenance of data. This will teach you how important it is to look at your data operations and administration before beginning the modeling of data.

Chapter 7, Scaling, shows you how powerful the autosharing characteristic of MongoDB can be, and how we think our data model is distributed.

Chapter 8, Logging and Real-time Analytics with MongoDB, takes you through an schema design of a real-life problem example.

What you need for this book

To successfully understand every chapter on this book, you need access to a MongoDB 3.0 instance.

You can choose where and how you will run it. We know that there are many ways you can do it. So, pick one.

To execute the queries and commands, I recommend you do this on a mongo shell. Every time I do this outside the mongo shell, I will warn you.

In *Chapter 8, Logging and Real-time Analytics with MongoDB*, you will need to have Node.js installed on your machine and it should have access to your MongoDB instance.

Who this book is for

This book assumes that you have already had first contact with MongoDB and have some experience with JavaScript. The book is for database administrators, developers, or anyone that is looking for some data modeling concepts and how they fit into the MongoDB world. It does not teach you JavaScript or how to install MongoDB on your machine. If you are a MongoDB beginner, you can find good Packt Publishing books that will help you to get enough experience to better understand this book.

Conventions

In this book, you will find a number of text styles that distinguish between different kinds of information. Here are some examples of these styles and an explanation of their meaning.

Code words in text, database table names, folder names, filenames, file extensions, pathnames, dummy URLs, user input, and Twitter handles are shown as follows: "We can store the relationship in the `Group` document."

A block of code is set as follows:

```
collection.update({resource: resource, date: today},
  {$inc : {daily: 1}}, {upsert: true},
  function(error, result){
    assert.equal(error, null);
    assert.equal(1, result.result.n);
    console.log("Daily Hit logged");
    callback(result);
});
```

When we wish to draw your attention to a particular part of a code block, the relevant lines or items are set in bold:

```
var logMinuteHit = function(db, resource, callback) {
  // Get the events collection
  var collection = db.collection('events');
  // Get current minute to update
  var currentDate = new Date();
  var minute = currentDate.getMinutes();
  var hour = currentDate.getHours();
  // We calculate the minute of the day
  var minuteOfDay = minute + (hour * 60);
  var minuteField = util.format('minute.%s', minuteOfDay);
```

Any command-line input or output is written as follows:

```
db.customers.find(
{"username": "johnclay"},
{_id: 1, username: 1, details: 1}
)
```

New terms and **important words** are shown in bold.

 Warnings or important notes appear in a box like this.

 Tips and tricks appear like this.

Reader feedback

Feedback from our readers is always welcome. Let us know what you think about this book — what you liked or disliked. Reader feedback is important for us as it helps us develop titles that you will really get the most out of.

To send us general feedback, simply e-mail feedback@packtpub.com, and mention the book's title in the subject of your message.

If there is a topic that you have expertise in and you are interested in either writing or contributing to a book, see our author guide at www.packtpub.com/authors.

Customer support

Now that you are the proud owner of a Packt book, we have a number of things to help you to get the most from your purchase.

Downloading the example code

You can download the example code files from your account at http://www.packtpub.com for all the Packt Publishing books you have purchased. If you purchased this book elsewhere, you can visit http://www.packtpub.com/support and register to have the files e-mailed directly to you.

Errata

Although we have taken every care to ensure the accuracy of our content, mistakes do happen. If you find a mistake in one of our books — maybe a mistake in the text or the code — we would be grateful if you could report this to us. By doing so, you can save other readers from frustration and help us improve subsequent versions of this book. If you find any errata, please report them by visiting http://www.packtpub.com/submit-errata, selecting your book, clicking on the **Errata Submission Form** link, and entering the details of your errata. Once your errata are verified, your submission will be accepted and the errata will be uploaded to our website or added to any list of existing errata under the Errata section of that title.

To view the previously submitted errata, go to https://www.packtpub.com/books/content/support and enter the name of the book in the search field. The required information will appear under the **Errata** section.

Piracy

Piracy of copyrighted material on the Internet is an ongoing problem across all media. At Packt, we take the protection of our copyright and licenses very seriously. If you come across any illegal copies of our works in any form on the Internet, please provide us with the location address or website name immediately so that we can pursue a remedy.

Please contact us at copyright@packtpub.com with a link to the suspected pirated material.

We appreciate your help in protecting our authors and our ability to bring you valuable content.

Questions

If you have a problem with any aspect of this book, you can contact us at questions@packtpub.com, and we will do our best to address the problem.

Introducing Data Modeling

1

Data modeling is a subject that has been discussed for a long time. Hence, various authors on the subject might have different views. Not so long ago, when the main discussions were focused on relational databases, data modeling was part of the process of data discovery and analysis in a domain. It was a holistic vision, where the final goal was to have a robust database able to support any kind of application.

Due to the flexibility of NoSQL databases, data modeling has been an inside out process, where you need to have previously understood an application's needs or performance characteristics to have a good data model at the end.

In this chapter, we will provide a brief history of the data modeling process over the years, showing you important concepts. We are going to cover the following topics:

- The relationship between MongoDB and NoSQL
- Introducing NoSQL
- Database design

The relationship between MongoDB and NoSQL

If you search on Google for MongoDB, you will find about 10,900,000 results. In a similar manner, if you check Google for NoSQL, no fewer than 13,000,000 results will come to you.

Now, on Google Trends, a tool that shows how often a term is searched relative to all searched terms globally, we can see that the growth of interest in both subjects is quite similar:

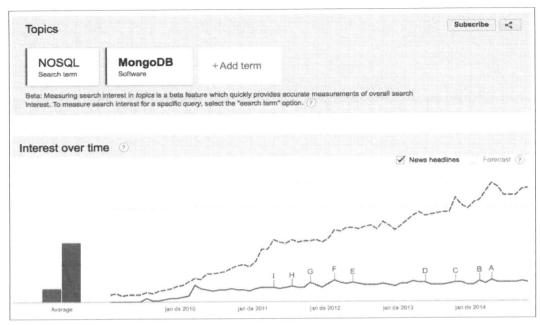

Google Trends search comparison between NoSQL and MongoDB terms since 2009

But, what actually exists in this relationship, besides the fact that MongoDB is a NoSQL database?

Since the first open source release in 2009, by a company named 10gen, MongoDB was the choice for many players on the Web and accordingly DB-Engines (http://db-engines.com/en/) became the fourth most popular database, and the most popular NoSQL database system.

10gen converted to MongoDB Inc. on August 27, 2013, showing that all eyes were on MongoDB and its ecosystem. The shift to an open source project was crucial in this change process. Especially, since the community adoption has been tremendous.

According to Dwight Merriman, the current chairman and co-founder of MongoDB:

> *"Our open source platform has resulted in MongoDB being downloaded 8 million times within the five years since the project has been available – that's an extremely fast pace for community adoption."*

Furthermore, MongoDB Inc. launched products and services to support this community and enrich the MongoDB ecosystem. Among them are:

- **MongoDB Enterprise**: A commercial support for MongoDB
- **MongoDB Management Service**: A SaaS monitoring tool
- **MongoDB University**: An EdX partnership that offers free—yes, it's free—online training

In the same way the NoSQL movement followed the growth of MongoDB, to meet both the challenges and opportunities of what might be referred to as Web 2.0, the NoSQL movement has grown substantially.

Introducing NoSQL (Not Only SQL)

Although the concept is new, NoSQL is a highly controversial subject. If you search widely, you may find many different explanations. As we do not have any intention of creating a new one, let's take a look at the most commonly-used explanation.

The term NoSQL, as we know today, was introduced by Eric Evans, after a meet up, organized by Johan Oskarsson from Last.fm.

Indeed, Oskarsson and everyone else who joined that historical meeting in San Francisco, on June 11, 2009, were already discussing many of the databases that today we call NoSQL databases, such as Cassandra, HBase, and CouchDB. As Oskarsson had described, the meeting was about open source, distributed, non-relational databases, for anyone who had "… run into limitations with traditional relational databases…," with the aim of "… figuring out why these newfangled Dynamo clones and BigTables have become so popular lately."

Four months later, Evans wrote in his weblog that, besides the growth of the NoSQL movement and everything that was being discussed, he thought they were going nowhere. However, Emil Eifren, the Neo4J founder and CEO, was right in naming the term as "Not Only SQL."

Emil Eifrem post on Twitter introducing the term "Not Only SQL"

More important than giving a definition to the term NoSQL, all these events were a starting point from which to discuss what NoSQL really is. Nowadays, there seems to be a general understanding that NoSQL was born as a response to every subject that relational databases were not designed to address.

Notably, we can now distinguish the problems that information systems must solve from the 70's up until today. At that time, monolithic architectures were enough to supply demand, unlike what we observe nowadays.

Have you ever stopped to think how many websites, such as social networks, e-mail providers, streaming services, and online games, you already have an account with? And, how many devices inside your house are connected to the Internet right now?

Do not worry if you cannot answer the preceding questions precisely. You are not alone. With each new research project, the number of users with Internet access around the globe increases, and the share that represents mobile internet access is more significant too.

This means that a large volume of unstructured or semi-structured data is generated every second, everywhere. The amount of data cannot be estimated, since the user is the main source of information. Thus, it is getting more and more difficult to predict when or why this volume will vary. It's just a matter of an unpredictable event happening somewhere in the world—such as a goal score, a general strike, a mass demonstration, or a plane crash—to have a variation on traffic, and consequently a growth of content generated by users.

In response to this, the development of NoSQL technology brought a variety of different approaches.

NoSQL databases types

As previously stated, Amazon Inc. and Google are at the forefront of NoSQL development with the help of Amazon DynamoDB and Google BigTable. Because of the diversity of styles, we have new types of NoSQL databases that are developed all the time. However, four basic types, based on data model, are known: key-value stores, wide-column stores, document databases, and graph databases, which are explained as follows:

- **Key-value stores**: The key-value is one of the most simple and straightforward data models, where each record is stored as a key together with its value. Examples of key-value stores are Amazon Dynamo, Riak, and Redis.

 Redis can be described as an advanced key-value cache and store. Since its keys can store many different data types and run atomic operations on these types, we may assume Redis to be a data structure server.

- **Wide-column stores**: Conceptually, the closest to relational databases, since its data is represented in a table. Nevertheless, the database stores columns of data instead of rows. Examples of wide-column stores are Google BigTable, Cassandra, and HBase.

- **Document databases**: As its name suggests, the data model of this database has as a main concept, the document. Documents are complex structures that store data as key-values, and can contain many key-value pairs, key-array pairs, or even nested documents. Examples of document databases are MongoDB, Apache CouchDB, and Amazon SimpleDB.

- **Graph databases**: Graph databases are the best way to store items of data whose relationships are best represented as graphs, such as network topologies and social networks. Nodes, edges, and properties are the structure of stored data. Examples of graph databases are Neo4J and HyperGraphDB.

Dynamic schema, scalability, and redundancy

Although, as explained earlier, NoSQL database types are based on different data models, they have some common features.

In order to support unstructured or semi-structured data, NoSQL databases have no predefined schema. The dynamic schema makes real-time changes simpler when inserting new data, and more cost-effective when data migration is needed.

To handle an unpredictable, large volume of data, NoSQL databases use auto-sharding to scale horizontally and ensure continuous availability of data. Auto-sharding allows users to automatically spread data and traffic across a number of servers.

NoSQL databases also support replication natively, which gives you high availability and recovery in a quick and easy way. As we distribute our data more and our recovery strategies change, we may fine-tune our consistency levels.

Database design and data modeling

Before I started to write this chapter (or maybe before beginning to write this book) I thought about how to deal with this subject. Firstly, because I would guess this was one of your expectations. Secondly, because this is a subject that is present in almost every literature, and I do not want to (and do not intend to) inflame this discussion.

The truth is that the discussion towards the theory versus practice, and until now in my life, I have favored the practical side. Therefore, I investigated, searched many different sources where I could read more about the subject, and maybe bring to this book a summary of everything that has been written until now on this subject.

Much that I have found at the beginning of my research showed me a clear separation between database design and data modeling. However, in the end, my conclusion was that both concepts have more similarities than divergences. And, to reach this conclusion, I had as stating point a fact mentioned by C.J. Date in *An Introduction to Database Systems, Pearson Education*.

In it, C.J. Date says that he prefers not to use the term data modeling because it could be refer to the term data model, and this relation may cause a little confusion. C.J. Date reminds us that the term data model has two meanings in the literature. The first is that a data model is a model of data in general, the second is that a data model is a model of persistent data relating to a specific enterprise. Date has chosen the first definition in his book.

As C.J. Date stated:

> *"We believe that the right way to do database design in a nonrelational system is to do a clean relation design first, and then, as a separate and subsequent step, to map that relational design into whatever nonrelational structures (for example. hierarchies) the target DBMS happens to support."*

Therefore, talking about database design is a good start. So, C.J. Date adopted the term semantic modeling, or conceptual modeling, and defined this activity as an aid in the process of database design.

 If you want to know more, you can find it in *An Introduction to Database Systems, 8th Edition, Chapter 14, page 410.*

Another important source that I found, which in some way complements the C.J. Date argumentation, is publications made by Graeme Simsion on *The Data Administration Newsletter*, http://www.tdan.com and in the book *Data Modeling: Theory and Practice*, Technics Publications LLC. Graeme Simsion is a data modeler, author of two data modeling books, and a researcher at Melbourne University.

In the vast majority of publications Simsion addresses the database design and data modeling subjects and concludes that data modeling is a discipline of database design and, consequently, the data model is the single and most important component of the design.

We notice that, unlike C.J. Date, Graeme Simsion uses the term data modeling.

In one of this publications, Simsion brings us an important fact regarding the data modeling concepts as a part of the process of database design. He talks about the stages of database design and tries to explain it by using some historic facts, and by a research with people who are directly involved with data modeling.

From the historic point of view, he mentioned the importance of 3-schema architecture on the evolution of data modeling concepts.

To understand this evolution, we have to go back in time to 1975. In that year, the Standards Planning and Requirements Committee of the American National Standards Institute also known as ANSI/SPARC/X3 Study Group on Data Base Management Systems, led by Charles Bachman, published a report proposing a DBMS architecture.

This report introduced an abstract architecture of DBMS that would be applicable for any data model—that is, a way that multiples the user's views and perceives the data.

The 3-schema architecture was developed to describe a final product, a database, not the process to design one. However, as previously mentioned, the 3-schema architecture introduced concepts that directly impact on the database design process including data modeling. In the next section we will go through the 3-schema architecture concepts to better understand data modeling concepts.

The ANSI-SPARC architecture

The ANSI-SPARC architecture proposed using three views (or three schemas) in order to:

- Hide the physical storage implementation from the user
- Ensure that the DBMS will give users access to the same data consistently, which means all users have with their own view
- Allow the database administrator to change something in the physical level without affecting the user's view

The external level

The external level, also known as the user view, details how each particular user sees the database. This level allows each user to view the data in a different way. For that reason, it is also the appropriate level to keep information about a user's specific requirements. The external schema describes how a database is structured for different user views. So, we can have many external schemas for a database.

The conceptual level

The conceptual level, despite being considered by many as the most important level, was the last level to arise in the architecture. This level aims to show how a database is logically structured. We can say that it is an abstract view of the data stored within the database.

The conceptual level acts as a layer between the user view and the database implementation. Therefore, in this level, details about the physical implementation and particularities about user views are not considered.

Once conceptual level is here, the database administrator has an important role in this architecture level where we have a database global view. It is their responsibility to define the logical structure.

A very interesting thing about the conceptual level is that we have to keep in mind that this level is independent from hardware or software. The conceptual schema defines the logical data structure as well as the relationships between the data in the database.

The internal level

The internal level represents how the data is stored. This schema defines physical storage structures such as indexes, data fields, and representations. There is only one internal schema for a database, but it is possible that there are many internal schemas for a conceptual schema.

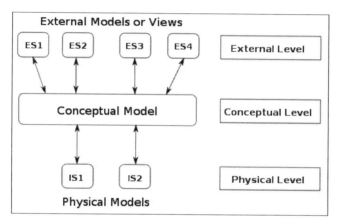

The ANSI/SPARC/X3 database architecture

The introduction of the concepts demonstrated by Charles Bachman and the ANSI/SPARC/X3 members were very meaningful. They brought a new way to see the database and introduced concepts that helped to develop the data modeling discipline.

Data modeling

As we stated before, data modeling can no longer be seen as a separate process. It is a stage in the database design process and a step that has to be done together with a business analysis. As the final result of the modeling process, we should have the logical data model.

This modeling process raises the controversial question of which approach we use. The core of this discussion deals with what is academic or what we see in practice.

To Matthew West and Julian Fowler, one way to see the modeling process is shown in the following diagram:

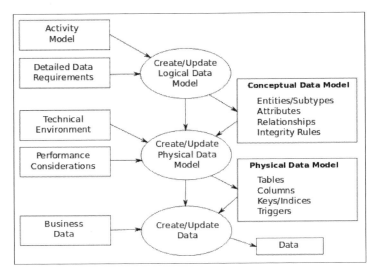

The data modeling process

Graeme Simsion has an entire article about this discussion. The article shows how the academic view of the modeling process is different than the real-life view. Both give names to the modeling stages, which are quite different.

During the writing process of this chapter, I am trying to present not only the Simsion research but also everything I have been through since I started working with information systems, in conjunction with extensive research about the modeling concepts, along with the countless views that I saw in many other sources.

Moreover, as previously stated, and also observed by Simsion, the three schema ANSI-SPARC architecture played a key role in the formation of the base concepts we have today. With the dissemination of the relational model and the DBMS based on it, the need to support old database architectures such as hierarchical and network-based has passed. Nevertheless, the way we divide the modeling process in two stages, one reflecting concepts very close to user views and followed by an automatic translation to a conceptual schema, remained.

We can say that the stages of the data modeling process we know nowadays came from the 3-schema architecture. Not only on the concepts, but also the names we use to noun each stage.

Hence, we most commonly find three types of data models: the conceptual model, logical model, and physical model.

The conceptual model

The conceptual model is a map of the entities and relationships with some attributes to illustrate. This is a high-level, abstract view, with the objective of identifying the fundamental concepts, very close to how users perceive the data, not focusing on a particular idea of the business.

If our audience is the business guys, that is the right model. It is frequently used to describe universal domain concepts, and should be DBMS-independent. For instance, we can mention entities such as person, store, product, instructor, student, and course.

Both in academic literature and in practice, the use of a relational notation is widely used to represent the conceptual model, even though the target implementation is not a relational DBMS. Indeed, this is a good approach to follow, as C.J. Date stated.

A common graphical representation of the conceptual model is the popular "crow's foot notation".

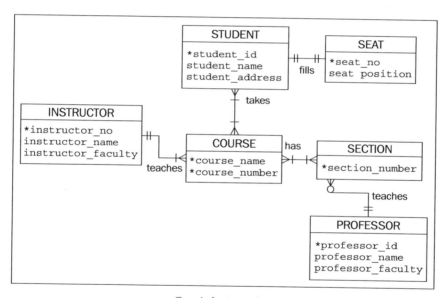

Crow's foot notation

It is often said that it is best practice to limit the conceptual model to printing on one page. The conceptual model can be a diagram or just a document describing everything you have identified.

The logical model

The logical model is the one that will be more business-friendly. This model should also be DBMS-independent, and is derived from the conceptual model.

It is common to describe business requirements in this model. Consequently, at this time, the data modeler will focus more on the project's scope. Details such as cardinality and nullability of relationship attributes with data types and constraints are mapped on this model too. As well as the conceptual model, is common to use a relational notation to represent the logical model. A data modeler has to work more on the logical model. This is because the logical model is where the modeler will explore all his possibilities and different ideas.

Generally, the logical model is a graphical presentation. The most widely used is the **entity-relationship (ER)** model, presented by Peter Chen in 1976. The ER model has a graphical notation that fits all the needs of a logical model.

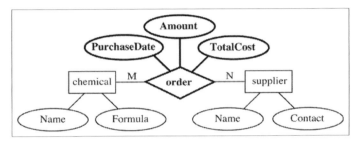

An entity-relationship diagram

The physical model

The physical model is a model where we have more detailed and less generic information about the data. In this model, we should know which technology should be used. Here, we can include tables, column names, keys, indexes, security roles, validation rules, and whatever detail you as a data modeler think is necessary.

Just to make the connection to the three-schema architecture clear, the physical model is in some way linked to the internal level on the architecture because it is in this level that we deal with how the stored data is represented to the user. The goal of this stage is to have an implemented database.

Summary

Data modeling is an important step in the database design process. There are many ways to ensure high quality in this process by involving all stakeholders. You will probably have a better knowledge of your data after modeling it.

That being said, we should always think about our data, and use a technique to model it.

In this chapter, you saw the history of NoSQL and also explored database designs and data modeling as a whole. We reviewed database architectures and you also learned about conceptual, logical, and physical models.

Now that you know more about data modeling, we will go through the MongoDB data model and the application of these concepts in the next chapter.

Data Modeling with MongoDB

2

Data modeling is a very important process during the conception of an application since this step will help you to define the necessary requirements for the database's construction. This definition is precisely the result of the data understanding acquired during the data modeling process.

As previously described, this process, regardless of the chosen data model, is commonly divided into two phases: one that is very close to the user's view and the other that is a translation of this view to a conceptual schema. In the scenario of relational database modeling, the main challenge is to build a robust database from these two phases, with the aim of guaranteeing updates to it with any impact during the application's lifecycle.

A big advantage of NoSQL compared to relational databases is that NoSQL databases are more flexible at this point, due to the possibility of a schemaless model that, in theory, can cause less impact on the user's view if a modification in the data model is needed.

Despite the flexibility NoSQL offers, it is important to previously know how we will use the data in order to model a NoSQL database. It is a good idea not to plan the data format to be persisted, even in a NoSQL database. Moreover, at first sight, this is the point where database administrators, quite used to the relational world, become more uncomfortable.

Relational database standards, such as SQL, brought us a sense of security and stability by setting up rules, norms, and criteria. On the other hand, we will dare to state that this security turned database designers distant of the domain from which the data to be stored is drawn.

The same thing happened with application developers. There is a notable divergence of interests among them and database administrators, especially regarding data models.

The NoSQL databases practically bring the need for an approximation between database professionals and the applications, and also the need for an approximation between developers and databases.

For that reason, even though you may be a data modeler/designer or a database administrator, don't be scared if from now on we address subjects that are out of your comfort zone. Be prepared to start using words common from the application developer's point of view, and add them to your vocabulary. This chapter will present the MongoDB data model along with the main concepts and structures available for the development and maintenance of this model.

This chapter will cover the following:

- Introducing your documents and collections
- The document's characteristics and structure
- Showing the document's design and patterns

Introducing documents and collections

MongoDB has the document as a basic unity of data. The documents in MongoDB are represented in **JavaScript Object Notation (JSON)**.

Collections are groups of documents. Making an analogy, a collection is similar to a table in a relational model and a document is a record in this table. And finally, collections belong to a database in MongoDB.

The documents are serialized on disk in a format known as **Binary JSON (BSON)**, a binary representation of a JSON document.

An example of a document is:

```
{
   "_id": 123456,
   "firstName": "John",
   "lastName": "Clay",
   "age": 25,
   "address": {
      "streetAddress": "131 GEN. Almério de Moura Street",
      "city": "Rio de Janeiro",
      "state": "RJ",
      "postalCode": "20921060"
   },
   "phoneNumber":[
      {
```

```
        "type": "home",
        "number": "+5521 2222-3333"
    },
    {
        "type": "mobile",
        "number": "+5521 9888-7777"
    }
    ]
}
```

Unlike the relational model, where you must declare a table structure, a collection doesn't enforce a certain structure for a document. It is possible that a collection contains documents with completely different structures.

We can have, for instance, on the same `users` collection:

```
{
    "_id": "123456",
    "username": "johnclay",
    "age": 25,
    "friends":[
        {"username": "joelsant"},
        {"username": "adilsonbat"}
    ],
    "active": true,
    "gender": "male"
}
```

We can also have:

```
{
    "_id": "654321",
    "username": "santymonty",
    "age": 25,
    "active": true,
    "gender": "male",
    "eyeColor": "brown"
}
```

In addition to this, another interesting feature of MongoDB is that not just data is represented by documents. Basically, all user interactions with MongoDB are made through documents. Besides data recording, documents are a means to:

- Define what data can be read, written, and/or updated in queries
- Define which fields will be updated

- Create indexes
- Configure replication
- Query the information from the database

Before we go deep into the technical details of documents, let's explore their structure.

JSON

JSON is a text format for the open-standard representation of data and that is ideal for data traffic. To explore the JSON format deeper, you can check *ECMA-404 The JSON Data Interchange Standard* where the JSON format is fully described.

 JSON is described by two standards: ECMA-404 and RFC 7159. The first one puts more focus on the JSON grammar and syntax, while the second provides semantic and security considerations.

As the name suggests, JSON arises from the JavaScript language. It came about as a solution for object state transfers between the web server and the browser. Despite being part of JavaScript, it is possible to find generators and readers for JSON in almost all the most popular programming languages such as C, Java, and Python.

The JSON format is also considered highly friendly and human-readable. JSON does not depend on the platform chosen, and its specification are based on two data structures:

- A set or group of key/value pairs
- A value ordered list

So, in order to clarify any doubts, let's talk about objects. Objects are a non-ordered collection of key/value pairs that are represented by the following pattern:

```
{
    "key" : "value"
}
```

In relation to the value ordered list, a collection is represented as follows:

```
["value1", "value2", "value3"]
```

In the JSON specification, a value can be:

- A string delimited with " "
- A number, with or without a sign, on a decimal base (base 10). This number can have a fractional part, delimited by a period (.), or an exponential part followed by e or E
- Boolean values (true or false)
- A null value
- Another object
- Another value ordered array

The following diagram shows us the JSON value structure:

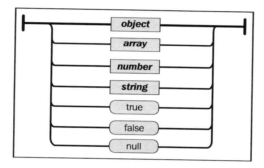

Here is an example of JSON code that describes a person:

```
{
    "name" : "Han",
    "lastname" : "Solo",
    "position" : "Captain of the Millenium Falcon",
    "species" : "human",
    "gender":"male",
    "height" : 1.8
}
```

BSON

BSON means **Binary JSON**, which, in other words, means binary-encoded serialization for JSON documents.

 If you are seeking more knowledge on BSON, I suggest you take a look at the BSON specification on http://bsonspec.org/.

If we compare BSON to the other binary formats, BSON has the advantage of being a model that allows you more flexibility. Also, one of its characteristics is that it's lightweight—a feature that is very important for data transport on the Web.

The BSON format was designed to be easily navigable and both encoded and decoded in a very efficient way for most of the programming languages that are based on C. This is the reason why BSON was chosen as the data format for MongoDB disk persistence.

The types of data representation in BSON are:

- String UTF-8 (`string`)
- Integer 32-bit (`int32`)
- Integer 64-bit (`int64`)
- Floating point (`double`)
- Document (`document`)
- Array (`document`)
- Binary data (`binary`)
- Boolean false (`\x00` or byte 0000 0000)
- Boolean true (`\x01` or byte 0000 0001)
- UTC datetime (`int64`)—the int64 is UTC milliseconds since the Unix epoch
- Timestamp (`int64`)—this is the special internal type used by MongoDB replication and sharding; the first 4 bytes are an increment, and the last 4 are a timestamp
- Null value ()
- Regular expression (`cstring`)
- JavaScript code (`string`)
- JavaScript code w/scope (`code_w_s`)
- Min key()—the special type that compares a lower value than all other possible BSON element values
- Max key()—the special type that compares a higher value than all other possible BSON element values
- ObjectId (`byte*12`)

Characteristics of documents

Before we go into detail about how we must model documents, we need a better understanding of some of its characteristics. These characteristics can determine your decision about how the document must be modeled.

The document size

We must keep in mind that the maximum length for a BSON document is 16 MB. According to BSON specifications, this length is ideal for data transfers through the Web and to avoid the excessive use of RAM. But this is only a recommendation. Nowadays, a document can exceed the 16 MB length by using GridFS.

 GridFS allows us to store documents in MongoDB that are larger than the BSON maximum size, by dividing it into parts, or chunks. Each chunk is a new document with 255 K of size.

Names and values for a field in a document

There are a few things that you must know about names and values for fields in a document. First of all, any field's name in a document is a string. As usual, we have some restrictions on field names. They are:

- The _id field is reserved for a primary key
- You cannot start the name using the character $
- The name cannot have a null character, or (.)

Additionally, documents that have indexed fields must respect the size limit for an indexed field. The values cannot exceed the maximum size of 1,024 bytes.

The document primary key

As seen in the preceding section, the _id field is reserved for the primary key. By default, this field must be the first one in the document, even when, during an insertion, it is not the first field to be inserted. In these cases, MongoDB moves it to the first position. Also, by definition, it is in this field that a unique index will be created.

The _id field can have any value that is a BSON type, except the array. Moreover, if a document is created without an indication of the _id field, MongoDB will automatically create an _id field of the ObjectId type. However, this is not the only option. You can use any value you want to identify your document as long as it is unique. There is another option, that is, generating an auto-incremental value based on a support collection or on an optimistic loop.

Support collections

In this method, we use a separate collection that will keep the last used value in the sequence. To increment the sequence, first we should query the last used value. After this, we can use the operator $inc to increment the value.

 There is a collection called system.js that can keep the JavaScript code in order to reuse it. Be careful not to include application logic in this collection.

Let's see an example for this method:

```
db.counters.insert(
    {
        _id: "userid",
        seq: 0
    }
)

function getNextSequence(name) {
    var ret = db.counters.findAndModify(
            {
                query: { _id: name },
                update: { $inc: { seq: 1 } },
                new: true
            }
    );
    return ret.seq;
}

db.users.insert(
    {
        _id: getNextSequence("userid"),
        name: "Sarah C."
    }
)
```

The optimistic loop

The generation of the _id field by an optimistic loop is done by incrementing each iteration and, after that, attempting to insert it in a new document:

```
function insertDocument(doc, targetCollection) {
    while (1) {
        var cursor = targetCollection.find( {},
        { _id: 1 } ).sort( { _id: -1 } ).limit(1);
        var seq = cursor.hasNext() ? cursor.next()._id + 1 : 1;
        doc._id = seq;
        var results = targetCollection.insert(doc);
        if( results.hasWriteError() ) {
            if( results.writeError.code == 11000 /* dup key */ )
                continue;
            else
                print( "unexpected error inserting data: " +
                tojson( results ) );
        }
        break;
    }
}
```

In this function, the iteration does the following:

1. Searches in `targetCollection` for the maximum value for _id.
2. Settles the next value for _id.
3. Sets the value on the document to be inserted.
4. Inserts the document.
5. In the case of errors due to duplicated _id fields, the loop repeats itself, or else the iteration ends.

 The points demonstrated here are the basics to understanding all the possibilities and approaches that this tool can offer. But, although we can use auto-incrementing fields for MongoDB, we must avoid using them because this tool does not scale for a huge data mass.

Designing a document

At this point, I believe you must be asking yourself: if the basic structure of the document is JSON (something so simple and textual), what can be so complex about the creation of a NoSQL database?

Let's see! First of all, yes! You are right. NoSQL databases can be very simple. But, this does not mean that their structure will be less complex than that of a relational database. It will be different, though!

As previously mentioned, collections do not force you to define the document's structure beforehand. But this is certainly a decision that you must make at some point. This decision will affect important aspects, especially in matters regarding a query's performance.

By now, you are likely to have also asked yourself how the applications represent a relationship between documents. If you did not think about this until now, it is not your fault. We are used to thinking about the relational world, such as wondering what the relationship is between a student and their classes or between a product and its orders.

MongoDB also has its own way of representing this kind of relationship. In fact, there are two ways:

- Embedded documents
- References

Working with embedded documents

Through the use of subdocuments, we can build more complex and optimized data structures. Thus, when we are modeling a document, we can choose to embed related data in one document.

The decision to embed data in one document is often related to the intention to get a better read performance, since with one query we can completely retrieve the information we need.

See the following example:

```
{
    id: 1,
    title: "MongoDB Data Modeling Blog post",
    body: "MongoDB Data Modeling....",
    author: "Wilson da Rocha França",
    date: ISODate("2014-11-19"),
    comments: [
        {
            name: "Mike",
            email : "mike@mike.com",
            comment: "Mike comment...."
        },
```

```
    {
        name: "Tom",
        email : "tom@tom.com",
        comment: "Tom comment...."
    },
    {
        name: "Yuri",
        email : "yuri@yuri.com",
        comment: "Yuri comment...."
    }
    ],
    tags: ["mongodb", "modeling", "nosql"]
}
```

As we can deduce, this document represents a blog post. The advantage of this kind of document is that, with a single query, we have all the data we need to present to the user. The same applies to updates: with just one query, we can modify the content of this document. Nevertheless, when we decide to embed data, we must ensure that the document does not exceed the BSON size limit of 16 MB.

There is no rule when embedding data in MongoDB, but overall, we should observe:

- Whether we have a one-to-one relationship between documents.
- Whether we have a one-to-many relationship between documents, and whether the "many" part of the relationship is very dependent of the "one" part. This means, for instance, that every time we present the "one" part, we will also present the "many" part of the relationship.

If our model fits in one of the preceding scenarios, we should consider using embedded documents.

Working with references

Normalization is a fundamental process to help build relational data models. In order to minimize redundancy, in this process we divide larger tables into smaller ones and define relationships among them. We can say that creating a reference in MongoDB is the way we have to "normalize" our model. This reference will describe the relationship between documents.

You may be confused about why we are considering relationships in a non-relational universe, even though this does not mean that relationships are not present in NoSQL databases. We will very often use the concepts of relational modeling to solve common problems. As stated before, to eliminate redundancy, documents can refer to each other.

But wait! There is something very important you should know from now on: MongoDB does not support joins. This means that, even with the reference to another document, you must perform at least two queries to get the complete information you need.

See the following example:

```
{
    _id: 1,
    name : "Product 1",
    description: "Product 1 description",
    price: "$10,00",
    supplier : {
        name: "Supplier 1",
        address: "St.1",
        telephone: "+552199999999"
    }
}

{
    _id: 2,
    name : "Product 2",
    description: "Product 2 description",
    price: "$10,00",
    supplier : {
        name: "Supplier 1",
        address: "St.1",
        telephone: "+552199999999"
    }
}

{
    _id: 3,
    name : "Product 3",
    description: "Product 3 description",
    price: "$10,00",
    supplier : {
        name: "Supplier 1",
        address: "St.1",
        telephone: "+552199999999"
    }
}
```

In the preceding example, we have documents from the `products` collection. We can see that, in the three products' instances, we have the same value for the supplier key. Instead of this repetition of data, we could have two collections: `products` and `suppliers`, as we can see in the following example:

```
suppliers

{
    _id: 1
    name: "Supplier 1",
    address: "St.1",
    telephone: "+552199999999",
    products: [1, 2, 3]
}

products

{
    _id: 1,
    name : "Product 1",
    description: "Product 1 description",
    price: "$10,00"
}

{
    _id: 2,
    name : "Product 2",
    description: "Product 2 description",
    price: "$10,00"
}

{
    _id: 3,
    name : "Product 3",
    description: "Product 3 description",
    price: "$10,00"
}
```

In this particular case, with a few products by the supplier, the choice to reference products based on the supplier is good. However, if the scenario were the opposite, a better approach would be:

```
suppliers

{
    _id: 1
    name: "Supplier 1",
    address: "St.1",
    telephone: "+552199999999"
}

products

{
    _id: 1,
    name : "Product 1",
    description: "Product 1 description",
    price: "$10,00",
    supplier: 1
}

{
    _id: 2,
    name : "Product 2",
    description: "Product 2 description",
    price: "$10,00",
    supplier: 1
}

{
    _id: 3,
    name : "Product 3",
    description: "Product 3 description",
    price: "$10,00",
    supplier: 1
}
```

There is no rule for references using MongoDB, but overall, we should observe:

- Whether we are duplicating the same information many times while embedding data (this shows poor reading performance)
- Whether we need to represent many-to-many relationships
- Whether our model is a hierarchy

If our model fits in one of the preceding scenarios, we should consider the use of references.

Atomicity

Another important concept that will affect our decisions when designing a document is atomicity. In MongoDB, operations are atomic at the document level. This means that we can modify one document at a time. Even if we have an operation that works in more than one document in a collection, this operation will happen in one document at a time.

Hence, when we decide to model a document with embedded data, we simply write operations, since all the data we need is in the same document. This is opposed to what happens when we choose to reference data, where we require many write operations that are not atomic.

Common document patterns

Now that we understood the way we can design our documents, let's take some examples of real-life problems, such as how to write a data model that better describes the relationship between entities.

This section will present you with patterns that illustrate when to embed or when to reference documents. Until now, we have considered as a deciding factor:

- Whether consistency is the priority
- Whether read is the priority
- Whether write is the priority
- What update queries we will make
- Document growth

One-to-one

One-to-one relationships are simpler than the others. Most of the time, we will map this relationship with embedded documents, especially if it is a "contains" relationship.

The following example shows a customer's document. In the first case, there is a reference in a `customerDetails` document; in the second, we see a reference with embedded data:

- Referenced data:

```
customer
{
    "_id": 5478329cb9617c750245893b
    "username" : "John Clay",
    "email": "johnclay@crgv.com",
    "password": "bf383e8469e98b44895d61b821748ae1"
}
customerDetails
{
    "customer_id": "5478329cb9617c750245893b",
    "firstName": "John",
    "lastName": "Clay",
    "gender": "male",
    "age": 25
}
```

- With embedded data:

```
customer
{
    _id: 1
    "username" : "John Clay",
    "email": "johnclay@crgv.com",
    "password": "bf383e8469e98b44895d61b821748ae1"
    "details": {
        "firstName": "John",
        "lastName": "Clay",
        "gender": "male",
        "age": 25
    }
}
```

The advantage of representing the relationship with an embedded document is that the customer detail data is always available when we query a customer. Thus, we can say that a customer's details do not make sense by themselves, only alongside the customer data.

One-to-many

One-to-many relationships are more complex than one-to-one relationships. In order to decide when to embed or to make references, we must consider the "many" side of the relationship. If the many side should be displayed with its parents, then we should choose to embed the data; otherwise, we can use references on the parents.

Let's see an example of customer and the customer's address:

```
customer
{
    _id: 1
    "username" : "John Clay",
    "email": "johnclay@crgv.com",
    "password": "bf383e8469e98b44895d61b821748ae1"
    "details": {
        "firstName": "John",
        "lastName": "Clay",
        "gender": "male",
        "age": 25
    }
}

address
{
    _id: 1,
    "street": "Address 1, 111",
    "city": "City One",
    "state": "State One",
    "type": "billing",
    "customer_id": 1
}
{
    _id: 2,
    "street": "Address 2, 222",
    "city": "City Two",
    "state": "State Two",
    "type": "shipping",
    "customer_id": 1
}
{
    _id: 3,
    "street": "Address 3, 333",
    "city": "City Three",
    "state": "State Three",
    "type": "shipping",
    "customer_id": 1
}
```

If, every time you want to display a customer's address, you also need to display the customer's name, then embedded documents are recommended:

```
customer
{
    _id: 1
    "username" : "John Clay",
    "email": "johnclay@crgv.com",
    "password": "bf383e8469e98b44895d61b821748ae1"
    "details": {
        "firstName": "John",
        "lastName": "Clay",
        "gender": "male",
        "age": 25
    }
    "billingAddress": [{
        "street": "Address 1, 111",
        "city": "City One",
        "state": "State One",
        "type": "billing",
    }],

    "shippingAddress": [{
        "street": "Address 2, 222",
        "city": "City Two",
        "state": "State Two",
        "type": "shipping"
    },
    {
        "street": "Address 3, 333",
        "city": "City Three",
        "state": "State Three",
        "type": "shipping"
    }]
}
```

Many-to-many

A many-to-many relationship is not something trivial, even in a relational universe. In the relational world, this kind of relationship is often represented as a join table while, in the non-relational one, it can be represented in many different ways.

In the following code, we will see a classic example of a `user` and `group` relation:

```
user

{
   _id: "5477fdea8ed5881af6541bf1",
   "username": "user_1",
   "password" : "3f49044c1469c6990a665f46ec6c0a41"
}

{
   _id: "54781c7708917e552d794c59",
   "username": "user_2",
   "password" : "15e1576abc700ddfd9438e6ad1c86100"
}

group

{
   _id: "54781cae13a6c93f67bdcc0a",
   "name": "group_1"
}

{
   _id: "54781d4378573ed5c2ce6100",
   "name": "group_2"
}
```

Now let's store the relationship in the `User` document:

```
user

{
   _id: "5477fdea8ed5881af6541bf1",
   "username": "user_1",
   "password" : "3f49044c1469c6990a665f46ec6c0a41",
   "groups": [
      {
         _id: "54781cae13a6c93f67bdcc0a",
         "name": "group_1"
      },
      {
         _id: "54781d4378573ed5c2ce6100",
         "name": "group_2"
      }
```

```
        ]
    }

    {
        _id: "54781c7708917e552d794c59",
        "username": "user_2",
        "password" : "15e1576abc700ddfd9438e6ad1c86100",
        "groups": [
            {
                _id: "54781d4378573ed5c2ce6100",
                "name": "group_2"
            }

        ]
    }

    group
    {
        _id: "54781cae13a6c93f67bdcc0a",
        "name": "group_1"
    }

    {
        _id: "54781d4378573ed5c2ce6100",
        "name": "group_2"
    }
```

Or we can store the relationship in the group document:

```
    user
    {
        _id: "5477fdea8ed5881af6541bf1",
        "username": "user_1",
        "password" : "3f49044c1469c6990a665f46ec6c0a41"
    }
    {
        _id: "54781c7708917e552d794c59",
        "username": "user_2",
        "password" : "15e1576abc700ddfd9438e6ad1c86100"
    }
    group
    {
        _id: "54781cae13a6c93f67bdcc0a",
        "name": "group_1",
        "users": [
```

```
        {
            _id: "54781c7708917e552d794c59",
            "username": "user_2",
            "password" : "15e1576abc700ddfd9438e6ad1c86100"
        }

    ]
}
{
    _id: "54781d4378573ed5c2ce6100",
    "name": "group_2",
    "users": [
        {
            _id: "5477fdea8ed5881af6541bf1",
            "username": "user_1",
            "password" :  "3f49044c1469c6990a665f46ec6c0a41"
        },
        {
            _id: "54781c7708917e552d794c59",
            "username": "user_2",
            "password" :  "15e1576abc700ddfd9438e6ad1c86100"
        }

    ]
}
```

And, finally, let's store the relationship in both documents:

```
user
{
    _id: "5477fdea8ed5881af6541bf1",
    "username": "user_1",
    "password" : "3f49044c1469c6990a665f46ec6c0a41",
    "groups": ["54781cae13a6c93f67bdcc0a",
    "54781d4378573ed5c2ce6100"]
}
{
    _id: "54781c7708917e552d794c59",
    "username": "user_2",
    "password" : "15e1576abc700ddfd9438e6ad1c86100",
    "groups": ["54781d4378573ed5c2ce6100"]
}
group
{
```

```
     _id: "54781cae13a6c93f67bdcc0a",
     "name": "group_1",
     "users": ["5477fdea8ed5881af6541bf1"]
}
{
     _id: "54781d4378573ed5c2ce6100",
     "name": "group_2",
     "users": ["5477fdea8ed5881af6541bf1",
     "54781c7708917e552d794c59"]
}
```

Summary

In this chapter, you saw how to build documents in MongoDB, examined their characteristics, and saw how they are organized into collections.

You now understand how important it is to already know the domain of the application in order to design the best models possible, and you saw some of the patterns that can help you to decide how to design your documents.

In the next chapter, we will see how to query these collections and modify the data that stored in them.

3
Querying Documents

In a NoSQL database, such as MongoDB, planning queries is a very important task, and depending on the query you want to perform, your document can vary greatly.

As you saw in *Chapter 2*, *Data Modeling with MongoDB*, the decision to refer or include documents in a collection is, in a large part, the result of our planning. It is essential to determine whether we will give a preference to reading or writing in a collection.

Here, we will see how planning queries can help us create documents in a more efficient and effective way, and we will also consider more sensible questions such as atomicity and transactions.

This chapter will focus on the following subjects:

- Read operations
- Write operations
- Write concerns
- Bulk writing documents

Understanding the read operations

Read is the most common and fundamental operation in a database. It's very hard to imagine a database that is used only to write information, where this information is never read. By the way, I have never heard of such an approach.

In MongoDB, we can execute queries through the `find` interface. The `find` interface can accept queries as criteria and projections as parameters. This will result in a cursor. Cursors have methods that can be used as modifiers of the executed query, such as `limit`, `map`, `skip`, and `sort`. For example, take a look at the following query:

```
db.customers.find({"username": "johnclay"})
```

This would return the following document:

```
{
    "_id" : ObjectId("54835d0ff059b08503e200d4"),
    "username" : "johnclay",
    "email" : "johnclay@crgv.com",
    "password" : "bf383e8469e98b44895d61b821748ae1",
    "details" : {
        "firstName" : "John",
        "lastName" : "Clay",
        "gender" : "male",
        "age" : 25
    },
    "billingAddress" : [
        {
            "street" : "Address 1, 111",
            "city" : "City One",
            "state" : "State One"
        }
    ],
    "shippingAddress" : [
        {
            "street" : "Address 2, 222",
            "city" : "City Two",
            "state" : "State Two"
        },
        {
            "street" : "Address 3,333",
            "city" : "City Three",
            "state" : "State Three"
        }
    ]
}
```

We can use the `find` interface to execute a query in MongoDB. The `find` interface will select the documents in a collection and return a cursor for the selected documents.

Compared with the SQL language, the `find` interface should be seen as a `select` statement. And, similar to a `select` statement where we can determinate clauses with expressions and predicates, the `find` interface allows us to use criteria and projections as parameters.

As mentioned before, we will use JSON documents in these `find` interface parameters. We can use the `find` interface in the following way:

```
db.collection.find(
  {criteria},
  {projection}
)
```

In this example:

- `criteria` is a JSON document that will specify the criteria for the selection of documents inside a collection by using some operators
- `projection` is a JSON document that will specify which document's fields in a collection will be returned as the query result

Both are optional parameters, and we will go into more detail regarding these later.

Let's execute the following example:

```
db.customers.find(
{"username": "johnclay"},
{_id: 1, username: 1, details: 1}
)
```

In this example:

- `{"username": "johnclay"}` is the criteria
- `{_id: 1, username: 1, details: 1}` is the projection

This query will result in this document:

```
{
   "_id" : ObjectId("54835d0ff059b08503e200d4"),
   "username" : "johnclay",
   "details" : {
   "firstName" : "John",
      "lastName" : "Clay",
      "gender" : "male",
      "age" : 25
   }
}
```

Selecting all documents

As mentioned in the previous section, in the find interface, both the criteria and projection parameters are optional. To use the find interface without any parameters means selecting all the documents in a collection.

 Note that the query result is a cursor with all the selected documents.

So, a query in the products collection executes in this way:

```
db.products.find()
```

It will return:

```
{
    "_id" : ObjectId("54837b61f059b08503e200db"),
    "name" : "Product 1",
    "description" : "Product 1 description",
    "price" : 10,
    "supplier" : {
        "name" : "Supplier 1",
        "telephone" : "+552199998888"
    }
}
{
    "_id" : ObjectId("54837b65f059b08503e200dc"),
    "name" : "Product 2",
    "description" : "Product 2 description",
    "price" : 20,
    "supplier" : {
        "name" : "Supplier 2",
        "telephone" : "+552188887777"
    }
}
...
```

Selecting documents using criteria

Despite the convenience, selecting all the documents in a collection can turn out to be a bad idea due to a given collection's length. If we take as an example a collection with hundreds, thousands, or millions of records, it is essential to create a criterion in order to select only the documents we want.

However, nothing prevents the query result from being huge. In this case, depending on the chosen drive that is executing the query, we must iterate the returned cursor.

 Note that in the mongo shell, the default value of returned records is 20.

Let's check the following example query. We want to select the documents where the attribute name is `Product 1`:

```
db.products.find({name: "Product 1"});
```

This will give us as a result:

```
{
    "_id" : ObjectId("54837b61f059b08503e200db"),
    "name" : "Product 1",
    "description" : "Product 1 description",
    "price" : 10,
    "supplier" : {
        "name" : "Supplier 1",
        "telephone" : "+552199998888"
    }
}
```

The preceding query selects the documents through the equality `{name: "Product 1"}`. It's also possible to use operators on the criteria interface.

The following example demonstrates how it's possible to select all documents where the price is greater than 10:

```
db.products.find({price: {$gt: 10}});
```

This produces as a result:

```
{
    "_id" : ObjectId("54837b65f059b08503e200dc"),
    "name" : "Product 2",
    "description" : "Product 2 description",
    "price" : 20,
    "supplier" : {
        "name" : "Supplier 2",
        "telephone" : "+552188887777"
    }
}
{
    "_id" : ObjectId("54837b69f059b08503e200dd"),
    "name" : "Product 3",
    "description" : "Product 3 description",
    "price" : 30,
    "supplier" : {
        "name" : "Supplier 3",
        "telephone" : "+552177776666"
    }
}
```

When we execute a query using the operator $gt, only documents that have an information price greater than 10 will be returned as a result in the cursor.

In addition, there are other operators such as comparison, logical, element, evaluation, geographical, and arrays.

Let's take, for example, the documents from the products collection, shown as follows:

```
{
    "_id" : ObjectId("54837b61f059b08503e200db"),
    "name" : "Product 1",
    "description" : "Product 1 description",
    "price" : 10,
    "supplier" : {
        "name" : "Supplier 1",
```

```
        "telephone" : "+552199998888"
    },
    "review" : [
        {
            "customer" : {
                "email" : "customer@customer.com"
        },
            "stars" : 5
        },
        {
            "customer" : {
                "email" : "customer2@customer.com"
            },
                "stars" : 6
            }
    ]
}
{
    "_id" : ObjectId("54837b65f059b08503e200dc"),
    "name" : "Product 2",
    "description" : "Product 2 description",
    "price" : 20,
    "supplier" : {
        "name" : "Supplier 2",
        "telephone" : "+552188887777"
    },
    "review" : [
        {
            "customer" : {
                "email" : "customer@customer.com"
            },
                "stars" : 10
        },
        {
            "customer" : {
                "email" : "customer2@customer.com"
```

```
            },
            "stars" : 2
        }
    ]
}
{
    "_id" : ObjectId("54837b69f059b08503e200dd"),
    "name" : "Product 3",
    "description" : "Product 3 description",
    "price" : 30,
    "supplier" : {
        "name" : "Supplier 3",
        "telephone" : "+552177776666"
    },
    "review" : [
        {
            "customer" : {
                "email" : "customer@customer.com"
            },
            "stars" : 5
        },
        {
            "customer" : {
                "email" : "customer2@customer.com"
            },
            "stars" : 9
        }
    ]
}
```

Comparison operators

MongoDB provides us with a way to define equality between values. With comparison operators, we can compare BSON type values. Let's look at these operators:

- The `$gte` operator is responsible for searching values that are equal or greater than the value specified in the query. If we execute the query `db.products.find({price: {$gte: 20}})`, it will return:

```
{
    "_id" : ObjectId("54837b65f059b08503e200dc"),
    "name" : "Product 2",
    "description" : "Product 2 description",
    "price" : 20,
    "supplier" : {
        "name" : "Supplier 2",
        "telephone" : "+552188887777"
    },
    "review" : [
        {
            "customer" : {
                "email" : "customer@customer.com"
            },
            "stars" : 10
        },
        {
            "customer" : {
                "email" : "customer2@customer.com"
            },
            "stars" : 2
        }
    ]
}
{
    "_id" : ObjectId("54837b69f059b08503e200dd"),
    "name" : "Product 3",
```

```
      "description" : "Product 3 description",
      "price" : 30,
      "supplier" : {
         "name" : "Supplier 3",
         "telephone" : "+552177776666"
      },
      "review" : [
         {
            "customer" : {
               "email" : "customer@customer.com"
            },
            "stars" : 5
         },
         {
            "customer" : {
               "email" : "customer2@customer.com"
            },
            "stars" : 9
         }
      ]
}
```

- With the `$lt` operator, it's possible to search for values that are inferior to the requested value in the query. The query `db.products.find({price: {$lt: 20}})` will return:

```
{
   "_id" : ObjectId("54837b61f059b08503e200db"),
   "name" : "Product 1",
   "description" : "Product 1 description",
   "price" : 10,
   "supplier" : {
      "name" : "Supplier 1",
      "telephone" : "+552199998888"
   },
   "review" : [
      {
         "customer" : {
```

```
            "email" : "customer@customer.com"
        },
        "stars" : 5
    },
    {
        "customer" : {
            "email" : "customer2@customer.com"
        },
        "stars" : 6
    }
    ]
}
```

- The `$lte` operator searches for values that are less than or equal to the requested value in the query. If we execute the query `db.products.find({price: {$lte: 20}})`, it will return:

```
{
    "_id" : ObjectId("54837b61f059b08503e200db"),
    "name" : "Product 1",
    "description" : "Product 1 description",
    "price" : 10,
    "supplier" : {
        "name" : "Supplier 1",
        "telephone" : "+552199998888"
    },
    "review" : [
        {
            "customer" : {
                "email" : "customer@customer.com"
            },
            "stars" : 5
        },
        {
            "customer" : {
                "email" : "customer2@customer.com"
            },
            "stars" : 6
```

```
        }
    ]
}
{
    "_id" : ObjectId("54837b65f059b08503e200dc"),
    "name" : "Product 2",
    "description" : "Product 2 description",
    "price" : 20,
    "supplier" : {
        "name" : "Supplier 2",
        "telephone" : "+552188887777"
    },
    "review" : [
        {
            "customer" : {
                "email" : "customer@customer.com"
            },
            "stars" : 10
        },
        {
            "customer" : {
                "email" : "customer2@customer.com"
            },
            "stars" : 2
        }
    ]
}
```

- The $in operator is able to search any document where the value of a field equals a value that is specified in the requested array in the query. The execution of the query db.products.find({price:{$in: [5, 10, 15]}}) will return:

```
{
    "_id" : ObjectId("54837b61f059b08503e200db"),
    "name" : "Product 1",
    "description" : "Product 1 description",
    "price" : 10,
```

```
        "supplier" : {
          "name" : "Supplier 1",
          "telephone" : "+552199998888"
        },
        "review" : [
            {
                "customer" : {
                    "email" : "customer@customer.com"
                },
                "stars" : 5
            },
            {
                "customer" : {
                    "email" : "customer2@customer.com"
                },
                "stars" : 6
            }
        ]
    }
```

- The $nin operator will match values that are not included in the specified array. The execution of the db.products.find({price:{$nin: [10, 20]}}) query will produce:

```
{
    "_id" : ObjectId("54837b69f059b08503e200dd"),
    "name" : "Product 3",
    "description" : "Product 3 description",
    "price" : 30,
    "supplier" : {
        "name" : "Supplier 3",
        "telephone" : "+552177776666"
    },
    "review" : [
        {
            "customer" : {
                "email" : "customer@customer.com"
            },
```

```
            "stars" : 5
        },
        {
            "customer" : {
                "email" : "customer2@customer.com"
            },
            "stars" : 9
        }
    ]
}
```

- The $ne operator will match any values that are not equal to the specified value in the query. The execution of the db.products.find({name: {$ne: "Product 1"}}) query will produce:

```
{
    "_id" : ObjectId("54837b65f059b08503e200dc"),
    "name" : "Product 2",
    "description" : "Product 2 description",
    "price" : 20,
    "supplier" : {
        "name" : "Supplier 2",
        "telephone" : "+552188887777"
    },
    "review" : [
        {
            "customer" : {
                "email" : "customer@customer.com"
            },
            "stars" : 10
        },
        {
            "customer" : {
                "email" : "customer2@customer.com"
            },
            "stars" : 2
        }
```

```
      ]
  }
  {
      "_id" : ObjectId("54837b69f059b08503e200dd"),
      "name" : "Product 3",
      "description" : "Product 3 description",
      "price" : 30,
      "supplier" : {
          "name" : "Supplier 3",
          "telephone" : "+552177776666"
      },
      "review" : [
          {
              "customer" : {
                  "email" : "customer@customer.com"
              },
              "stars" : 5
          },
          {
              "customer" : {
                  "email" : "customer2@customer.com"
              },
              "stars" : 9
          }
      ]
  }
```

Logical operators

Logical operators are how we define the logic between values in MongoDB. These
are derived from Boolean algebra, and the truth value of a Boolean value can be
either true or false. Let's look at the logical operators in MongoDB:

- The $and operator will make a logical *AND* operation in an expressions
  array, and will return the values that match all the specified criteria. The
  execution of the db.products.find({$and: [{price: {$lt: 30}},
  {name: "Product 2"}]}) query will produce:

```
{
    "_id" : ObjectId("54837b65f059b08503e200dc"),
    "name" : "Product 2",
```

```
        "description" : "Product 2 description",
        "price" : 20,
        "supplier" : {
            "name" : "Supplier 2",
            "telephone" : "+552188887777"
        },
        "review" : [
            {
                "customer" : {
                    "email" : "customer@customer.com"
                },
                "stars" : 10
            },
            {
                "customer" : {
                    "email" : "customer2@customer.com"
                },
                "stars" : 2
            }
        ]
    }
```

- The $or operator will make a logical *OR* operation in an expressions array, and will return all the values that match either of the specified criteria. The execution of the db.products.find({$or: [{price: {$gt: 50}}, {name: "Product 3"}]}) query will produce:

```
    {
        "_id" : ObjectId("54837b69f059b08503e200dd"),
        "name" : "Product 3",
        "description" : "Product 3 description",
        "price" : 30,
        "supplier" : {
            "name" : "Supplier 3",
            "telephone" : "+552177776666"
        },
        "review" : [
            {
```

```
        "customer" : {
            "email" : "customer@customer.com"
        },
        "stars" : 5
    },
    {
        "customer" : {
            "email" : "customer2@customer.com"
        },
        "stars" : 9
    }
  ]
}
```

- The $not operator inverts the query effect and returns the values that do not match the specified operator expression. It is used to negate any operation. The execution of the db.products.find({price: {$not: {$gt: 10}}}) query will produce:

```
{
    "_id" : ObjectId("54837b61f059b08503e200db"),
    "name" : "Product 1",
    "description" : "Product 1 description",
    "price" : 10,
    "supplier" : {
        "name" : "Supplier 1",
        "telephone" : "+552199998888"
    },
    "review" : [
        {
            "customer" : {
                "email" : "customer@customer.com"
            },
            "stars" : 5
        },
        {
            "customer" : {
                "email" : "customer2@customer.com"
```

```
        },
        "stars" : 6
    }
  ]
}
```

- The $nor operator will make a logical *NOR* operation in an expressions array, and will return all the values that fail to match all the specified expressions in the array. The execution of the `db.products.find({$nor:[{price:{$gt: 35}}, {price:{$lte: 20}}]})` query will produce:

```
{
    "_id" : ObjectId("54837b69f059b08503e200dd"),
    "name" : "Product 3",
    "description" : "Product 3 description",
    "price" : 30,
    "supplier" : {
        "name" : "Supplier 3",
        "telephone" : "+552177776666"
    },
    "review" : [
        {
            "customer" : {
                "email" : "customer@customer.com"
            },
            "stars" : 5
        },
        {
            "customer" : {
                "email" : "customer2@customer.com"
            },
            "stars" : 9
        }
    ]
}
```

Element operators

To query a collection about our documents fields, we can use element operators.

The $exists operator will return all documents that have the specified field in the query. The execution of db.products.find({sku: {$exists: true}}) will not return any document, because none of them have the field sku.

Evaluation operators

Evaluation operators are how we perform an assessment of an expression in MongoDB. We must take care with this kind of operator, especially if there is no index for the field we are using on the criteria. Let's consider the evaluation operator:

- The $regex operator will return all values that match a regular expression. The execution of db.products.find({name: {$regex: /2/}}) will return:

```
{
    "_id" : ObjectId("54837b65f059b08503e200dc"),
    "name" : "Product 2",
    "description" : "Product 2 description",
    "price" : 20,
    "supplier" : {
        "name" : "Supplier 2",
        "telephone" : "+552188887777"
    },
    "review" : [
        {
            "customer" : {
                "email" : "customer@customer.com"
            },
            "stars" : 10
        },
        {
            "customer" : {
                "email" : "customer2@customer.com"
            },
            "stars" : 2
        }
    ]
}
```

Array operators

When we are working with arrays on a query, we should use array operators. Let's consider the array operator:

- The `$elemMatch` operator will return all documents where the specified array field values have at least one element that match the query criteria conditions.

  The `db.products.find({review: {$elemMatch: {stars: {$gt: 5}, customer: {email: "customer@customer.com"}}}})` query will look at all the collection documents where the `review` field has documents, the `stars` field value is greater than 5, and `customer email` is `customer@customer.com`:

  ```
  {
      "_id" : ObjectId("54837b65f059b08503e200dc"),
      "name" : "Product 2",
      "description" : "Product 2 description",
      "price" : 20,
      "supplier" : {
          "name" : "Supplier 2",
          "telephone" : "+552188887777"
      },
      "review" : [
          {
              "customer" : {
                  "email" : "customer@customer.com"
              },
              "stars" : 10
          },
          {
              "customer" : {
                  "email" : "customer2@customer.com"
              },
              "stars" : 2
          }
      ]
  }
  ```

Besides the presented operators, we have: $mod, $text, $where, $all, $geoIntersects, $geoWithin, $nearSphere, $near, $size, and $comment. You can find more information regarding this in the MongoDB manual reference at http://docs.mongodb.org/manual/reference/operator/query/.

Projections

Until now, we have executed queries where the presented result is the document as it is persisted in MongoDB. But, in order to optimize the network overhead between MongoDB and its clients, we should use projections.

As you saw at the beginning of the chapter, the find interface allows us to use two parameters. The second parameter is projections.

By using the same sample collection we used in the previous session, an example of a query with projection would be:

```
db.products.find({price: {$not: {$gt: 10}}}, {name: 1, description: 1})
```

This query produces:

```
{
    "_id" : ObjectId("54837b61f059b08503e200db"),
    "name" : "Product 1",
    "description" : "Product 1 description"
}
```

The projection is a JSON document with all the fields we would like to present or hide, followed by 0 or 1, depending on what we want.

When a field is followed by a 0, then this field will not be shown in the resulting document. On the other hand, if the field is followed by a 1, then this means that it will be shown in the resulting document.

By default, the _id field has the value 1.

The db.products.find({price: {$not: {$gt: 10}}}, {_id: 0, name: 1, "supplier.name": 1}) query will show the following document:

```
{ "name" : "Product 1", "supplier" : { "name" : "Supplier 1" } }
```

In fields that have an array as a value, we can use operators such as $elemMatch, $split, $slice, and $.

The db.products.find({price: {$gt: 20}}, {review: {$elemMatch: {stars: 5}}}) query will produce:

```
{
    "_id" : ObjectId("54837b69f059b08503e200dd"),
    "review" : [
        {
            "customer" : {
                "email" : "customer@customer.com"
            },
            "stars" : 5
        }
    ]
}
```

Introducing the write operations

In MongoDB, we have three kinds of write operations: insert, update, and remove. To run these operations, MongoDB provides three interfaces: db.document.insert, db.document.update, and db.document.remove. The write operations in MongoDB are targeted to a specific collection and are atomic on the level of a single document.

The write operations are as important as the read operations when we are modeling documents in MongoDB. The atomicity in a level of a single document can determine whether we embed documents or not. We will go into this in a little more detail in *Chapter 7, Scaling*, but the activity of choosing a shard key will be decisive in whether we write an operation's performance because, depending on the key choice, we will write in one or many shards.

Also, another determining factor in a writing operations' performance is related to the MongoDB physical model. There are many recommendations given by 10gen but let's focus on those that have the greatest impact on our development. Due to MongoDB's update model, which is based on random I/O operations, it is recommended that you use solid state discs, or SSD. The solid state disk has superior performance compared to spinning disks, in terms of random I/O operations. Even though spinning disks are cheaper, and the cost to scale an infrastructure based on this kind of hardware is not that expensive either, the use of SSDs or increasing the RAM is still more effective. Studies on this subject show us that SSDs outperform spinning disks by 100 times for random I/O operations.

Another important thing to understand about write operations is how the documents are actually written on disk by MongoDB. MongoDB uses a journaling mechanism to write operations, and this mechanism uses a journal to write the change operation before we write it in the data files. This is very useful, especially when we have a dirty shutdown. MongoDB will use the journal files to recover the database state to a consistent state when the `mongod` process is restarted.

As stated in *Chapter 2, Data Modeling with MongoDB,* the BSON specification allows us to have a document with the maximum size of 16 MB. Since its 2.6 version, MongoDB uses a space allocation strategy for a record, or document, named "power of two sized allocation." As its name suggests, MongoDB will allocate to each document a size in bytes that is its size to the power of two (for example, 32, 64, 128, 256, 512, …), considering that the minimum size of a document is 32 bytes. This strategy allocates more space than the document really needs, giving it more space to grow.

Inserts

The `insert` interface is one of the possible ways of creating a new document in MongoDB. The `insert` interface has the following syntax:

```
db.collection.insert(
    <document or array of documents>,
    {
        writeConcern: <document>,
        ordered: <boolean>
    }
)
```

Here:

- `document or array of documents` is either a document or an array with one or many documents that should be created in the targeted collection.

- `writeConcern` is a document expressing the write concern.

- `ordered` should be a Boolean value, which if true will carry out an ordered process on the documents of the array, and if there is an error in a document, MongoDB will stop processing it. Otherwise, if the value is false, it will carry out an unordered process and it will not stop if an error occurs. By default, the value is `true`.

In the following example, we can see how an `insert` operation can be used:

```
db.customers.insert({
    username: "customer1",
    email: "customer1@customer.com",
    password: hex_md5("customer1paswd")
})
```

As we did not specify a value for the `_id` field, it will be automatically generated with a unique `ObjectId` value. The document created by this `insert` operation is:

```
{
    "_id" : ObjectId("5487ada1db4ff374fd6ae6f5"),
    "username" : "customer1",
    "email" : "customer1@customer.com",
    "password" : "b1c5098d0c6074db325b0b9dddb068e1"
}
```

As you observed in the first paragraph of this section, the `insert` interface is not the only way to create new documents in MongoDB. By using the `upsert` option on updates, we could also create new documents. Let's go into more detail regarding this now.

Updates

The `update` interface is used to modify previous existing documents in MongoDB, or even to create new ones. To select which document we would like to change, we will use a criterion. An update can modify the field values of a document or an entire document.

An update operation will modify only one document at a time. If the criterion matches more than one document, then it is necessary to pass a document with a `multi` parameter with the `true` value to the update interface. If the criteria matches no document and the `upsert` parameter is `true`, a new document will be created, or else it will update the matching document.

The `update` interface is represented as:

```
db.collection.update(
    <query>,
    <update>,
    {
```

```
    upsert: <boolean>,
    multi: <boolean>,
    writeConcern: <document>
}
)
```

Here:

- `query` is the criteria
- `update` is the document containing the modification to be applied
- `upsert` is a Boolean value that, if true, creates a new document if the criteria does not match any document in the collection
- `multi` is a Boolean value that, if true, updates every document that meets the criteria
- `writeConcern` is a document expressing the write concern

Using the document created in the previous session, a sample update would be:

```
db.customers.update(
    {username: "customer1"},
    {$set: {email: "customer1@customer1.com"}}
)
```

The modified document is:

```
{
    "_id" : ObjectId("5487ada1db4ff374fd6ae6f5"),
    "username" : "customer1",
    "email" : "customer1@customer1.com",
    "password" : "b1c5098d0c6074db325b0b9dddb068e1"
}
```

The $set operator allows us to update only the email field of the matched documents.

Otherwise, you may have this update:

```
db.customers.update(
    {username: "customer1"},
    {email: "customer1@customer1.com"}
)
```

In this case, the modified document would be:

```
{
    "_id" : ObjectId("5487ada1db4ff374fd6ae6f5"),
    "email" : "customer1@customer1.com"
}
```

That is, without the `$set` operator, we modify the old document with the one passed as a parameter on the update. Besides the `$set` operator, we also have other important update operators:

- `$inc` increments the value of a field with the specified value:

  ```
  db.customers.update(
      {username: "johnclay"},
      {$inc: {"details.age": 1}}
  )
  ```

  This update will increment the field `details.age` by 1 in the matched documents.

- `$rename` will rename the specified field:

  ```
  db.customers.update(
      {email: "customer1@customer1.com"},
      {$rename: {username: "login"}}
  )
  ```

  This update will rename the field `username` to `login` in the matched documents.

- `$unset` will remove the field from the matched document:

  ```
  db.customers.update(
      {email: "customer1@customer1.com"},
      {$unset: {login: ""}}
  )
  ```

  This update will remove the `login` field from the matched documents.

As the write operations are atomic at the level of a single document, we can afford to be careless with the use of the preceding operators. All of them can be safely used.

Write concerns

Many of the discussions surrounding non-relational databases are related to the ACID concept. We, as database professionals, software engineers, architects, and developers, are fairly accustomed to the relational universe, and we spend a lot of time developing without caring about ACID matters.

Nevertheless, we should understand by now why we really have to take this matter into consideration, and how these simple four letters are essential in the non-relational world. In this section, we will discuss the letter **D**, which means durability, in MongoDB.

Durability in database systems is a property that tells us whether a write operation was successful, whether the transaction was committed, and whether the data was written on non-volatile memory in a durable medium, such as a hard disk.

Unlike relational database systems, the response to a write operation in NoSQL databases is determined by the client. Once again, we have the possibility to make a choice on our data modeling, addressing the specific needs of a client.

In MongoDB, the response of a successful write operation can have many levels of guarantee. This is what we call a write concern. The levels vary from weak to strong, and the client determines the strength of guarantee. It is possible for us to have, in the same collection, both a client that needs a strong write concern and another that needs a weak one.

The write concern levels that MongoDB offers us are:

- Unacknowledged
- Acknowledged
- Journaled
- Replica acknowledged

Unacknowledged

As its name suggests, with an unacknowledged write concern, the client will not attempt to respond to a write operation. If this is possible, only network errors will be captured. The following diagram shows that drivers will not wait that MongoDB acknowledge the receipt of write operations:

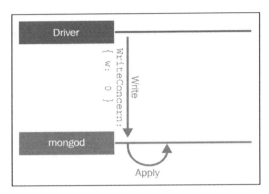

In the following example, we have an `insert` operation in the `customers` collection with an unacknowledged write concern:

```
db.customers.insert(

{username: "customer1", email: "customer1@customer.com", password: hex_
md5("customer1paswd")},

{writeConcern: {w: 0}}

)
```

Acknowledged

With this write concern, the client will have an acknowledgement of the write operation, and see that it was written on the in-memory view of MongoDB. In this mode, the client can catch, among other things, network errors and duplicate keys. Since the 2.6 version of MongoDB, this is the default write concern.

As you saw earlier, we can't guarantee that a write on the in-memory view of MongoDB will be persisted on the disk. In the event of a failure of MongoDB, the data in the in-memory view will be lost. The following diagram shows that drivers wait MongoDB acknowledge the receipt of write operations and applied the change to the in-memory view of data:

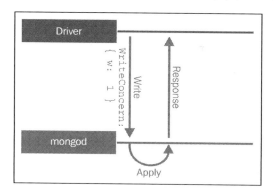

In the following example, we have an `insert` operation in the `customers` collection with an acknowledged write concern:

```
db.customers.insert(
{username: "customer1", email: "customer1@customer.com", password: hex_
md5("customer1paswd")},
{writeConcert: {w: 1}}
)
```

Journaled

With a journaled write concern, the client will receive confirmation that the write operation was committed in the journal. Thus, the client will have a guarantee that the data will be persisted on the disk, even if something happens to MongoDB.

To reduce the latency when we use a journaled write concern, MongoDB will reduce the frequency in which it commits operations to the journal from the default value of 100 milliseconds to 30 milliseconds. The following diagram shows that drivers will wait MongoDB acknowledge the receipt of write operations only after committing the data to the journal:

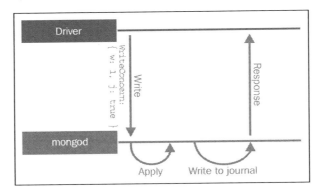

In the following example, we have an `insert` in the `customers` collection with a journaled write concern:

```
db.customers.insert(

{username: "customer1", email: "customer1@customer.com", password: hex_
md5("customer1paswd")},

{writeConcern: {w: 1, j: true}}

)
```

Replica acknowledged

When we are working with replica sets, it is important to be sure that a write operation was successful not only in the primary node, but also that it was propagated to members of the replica set. For this purpose, we use a replica acknowledged write concern.

By changing the default write concern to replica acknowledged, we can determine the number of members of the replica set from which we want the write operation confirmation. The following diagram shows that drivers will wait that MongoDB acknowledge the receipt of write operations on a specified number of the replica set members:

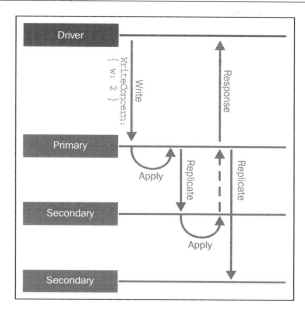

In the following example, we will wait until the write operation propagates to the primary and at least two secondary nodes:

```
db.customers.insert(
{username: "customer1", email: "customer1@customer.com", password: hex_
md5("customer1paswd")},
{writeConcern: {w: 3}}
)
```

We should include a timeout property in milliseconds to avoid that a write operation remains blocked in a case of a node failure.

In the following example, we will wait until the write operation propagates to the primary and at least two secondary nodes, with a timeout of three seconds. If one of the two secondary nodes from which we are expecting a response fails, then the method times out after three seconds:

```
db.customers.insert(
{username: "customer1", email: "customer1@customer.com", password: hex_
md5("customer1paswd")},
{writeConcern: {w: 3, wtimeout: 3000}}
)
```

Bulk writing documents

Sometimes it is quite useful to insert, update, or delete more than one record of your collection. MongoDB provides us with the capability to perform bulk write operations. A bulk operation works in a single collection, and can be either ordered or unordered.

As with the `insert` method, the behavior of an ordered bulk operation is to process records serially, and if an error occurs, MongoDB will return without processing any of the remaining operations.

The behavior of an unordered operation is to process in parallel, so if an error occurs, MongoDB will still process the remaining operations.

We also can determine the level of acknowledgement required for bulk write operations. Since its 2.6 version, MongoDB has introduced new bulk methods with which we can insert, update, or delete documents. However, we can make a bulk insert only by passing an array of documents on the `insert` method.

In the following example, we make a bulk insert using the `insert` method:

```
db.customers.insert(
[
{username: "customer3", email: "customer3@customer.com", password: hex_
md5("customer3paswd")},
{username: "customer2", email: "customer2@customer.com", password: hex_
md5("customer2paswd")},
{username: "customer1", email: "customer1@customer.com", password: hex_
md5("customer1paswd")}
]
)
```

In the following example, we make an unordered bulk insert using the new bulk methods:

```
var bulk = db.customers.initializeUnorderedBulkOp();
bulk.insert({username: "customer1", email: "customer1@customer.com",
password: hex_md5("customer1paswd")});
bulk.insert({username: "customer2", email: "customer2@customer.com",
password: hex_md5("customer2paswd")});
bulk.insert({username: "customer3", email: "customer3@customer.com",
password: hex_md5("customer3paswd")});
bulk.execute({w: "majority", wtimeout: 3000});
```

We should use all the power tools MongoDB provides us with, but not without paying all our possible attention. MongoDB has a limit of executing a maximum of 1,000 bulk operations at a time. So, if this limit is exceeded, MongoDB will divide the operations into groups of a maximum of 1,000 bulk operations.

Summary

In this chapter, you were hopefully able to better understand the read and write operations in MongoDB. Moreover, now, you should also understand why it is important that you already know the queries you need to execute even before the document modeling process. Finally, you learned how to use the MongoDB properties, such as atomicity, at the document level and saw how it can help us to produce better queries.

In the next chapter, you will see how a special data structure known as index can improve the execution of our queries.

4
Indexing

As you have seen with the subject of relational databases, indexes are important structures when we think of a performance boost. In fact, indexes are so important that for most database administrators, they are a critical tool in their search for the continuous improvement of database performance.

In NoSQL databases such as MongoDB, indexing is part of a bigger strategy that will allow us to achieve many gains in performance and assign important behaviors to our database, which will be essential to the data model's maintenance.

This happens because we can have indexes with very special properties in MongoDB. For example, we can define an index of a date typed field that will control when a document should be removed from the collection.

So, in this chapter we will see:

- Indexing documents
- Index types
- Special index properties

Indexing documents

Out of all the subjects we have been discussing in this book so far, this is where we will be the most at ease. The index concept is present in almost every relational database, so if you have any previous basic knowledge on the matter, you will most likely have no difficulty in this chapter.

But in case you feel that you are not familiar enough with the concept of indexes, an easy way to understand them is to draw a parallel with books. Suppose that we have a book with an index like this:

Index

A
About cordless telephones   51
Advanced operation   17
Answer an external call during an
    intercom call   15
Answering system operation   27

B
Basic operation   14
Battery   9, 38

C
Call log   22, 37
Call waiting   14
Chart of characters   18

D
Date and time   8
Delete from redial   26
Delete from the call log   24
Delete from the directory   20
Delete your announcement   32
Desk/table bracket installation   4
Dial a number from redial   26

Dial type   4, 12
Directory   17
DSL filter   5

E
Edit an entry in the directory   20
Edit handset name   11

F
FCC, ACTA and IC regulations   53
Find handset   16

H
Handset display screen messages   36
Handset layout   6

I
Important safety instructions   39
Index   56-57
Installation   1
Install handset battery   2
Intercom call   15
Internet   4

With this in hand, if we decide to read about the Internet, we know that on page **4**, we will find information on the subject. On the other hand, how would we be able to find information we are looking for without the page number? The answer is quite simple: by going through the entire book, page by page, until we find the word "Internet."

As you might already know, indexes are data structures that hold part of the data from our main data source. In relational databases, indexes hold parts of a table, while in MongoDB, since indexes are on a collection level, these will hold part of a document. Similar to relational databases, indexes use a B-Tree data structure at implementation level.

Depending on our application's requirements, we can create indexes of fields or fields of embedded documents. When we create an index, it will hold a sorted set of values of the fields we choose.

Thus, when we execute a query, if there is an index that covers the query criteria, MongoDB will use the index to limit the number of documents to be scanned.

We have the `customers` collection that we used in *Chapter 3, Querying Documents*, which contains these documents:

```
{
    "_id" : ObjectId("54aecd26867124b88608b4c9"),
    "username" : "customer1",
    "email" : "customer1@customer.com",
    "password" : "b1c5098d0c6074db325b0b9dddb068e1"
}
```

We can create an index in the mongo shell on the `username` field, by using the `createIndex` method:

```
db.customers.createIndex({username: 1})
```

The following query will use the previously created index:

```
db.customers.find({username: "customer1"})
```

> Since Version 3.0.0, the `ensureIndex` method is deprecated and is an alias for the `createIndex` method.

We could state that this is the simplest way to create and use an index in MongoDB. In addition to this, we can create indexes on multikey fields or in embedded documents' fields, for instance.

In the next section, we will go through all these index types.

Indexing a single field

As we already stated in the last section, the simplest way to create an index on MongoDB is to do so in a single field. The index could be created on a field of any type in the collection of documents.

Consider the `customers` collection we used before, with some modification to work in this section:

```
{
    "_id" : ObjectId("54aecd26867124b88608b4c9"),
    "username" : "customer1",
```

```
"email" : "customer1@customer.com",
"password" : "b1c5098d0c6074db325b0b9dddb068e1",
"age" : 25,
"address" : {

    "street" : "Street 1",
    "zipcode" : "87654321",
    "state" : "RJ"


}
}
```

The following command creates an ascending index in the username field:

```
db.customers.createIndex({username: 1})
```

In order to create an index in MongoDB, we use the createIndex method. In the preceding code, we just passed a single document as a parameter to the createIndex method. The document {username: 1} contains a reference to the field that the index should be creating and the order: 1 for ascending or -1 for descending.

Another way to create the same index, but in descending order, is:

```
db.customers.createIndex({username: -1})
```

In the following query, MongoDB will use the index created in the username field to reduce the number of documents in the customers collection that it should inspect:

```
db.customers.find({username: "customer1"})
```

Besides the creation of indexes on a string or the number fields in the collection document, we could create an index of a field in an embedded document. Therefore, queries such as this will use the created index:

```
db.customers.createIndex({"address.state": 1})
```

The following code creates an index of the state field of the embedded address document:

```
db.customers.find({"address.state": "RJ"})
```

While a bit more complex, we can also create an index of the entire embedded document:

```
db.customers.createIndex({address: 1})
```

The following query will use the index:

```
db.customers.find(
{
    "address" :
    {
        "street" : "Street 1",
        "zipcode" : "87654321",
        "state" : "RJ"
    }
}
)
```

But none of these queries will do this:

```
db.customers.find({state: "RJ"})
```

```
db.customers.find({address: {zipcode: "87654321"}})
```

This happens because in order to match an embedded document, we have to match exactly the entire document, including the field order. The following query will not use the index either:

```
db.customers.find(
{
    "address" :
    {
        "state" : "RJ",
        "street" : "Street 1",
        "zipcode" : "87654321"
    }
}
)
```

Although the document contains all the fields, these are in a different order.

Before moving on to the next type of index, let's review a concept that you learned in *Chapter 3, Querying Documents*, the _id field. For every new document created in a collection, we should specify the _id field. If we do not specify it, MongoDB automatically creates one ObjectId typed for us. Furthermore, every collection automatically creates a unique ascending index of the _id field. That being said, we can state that the _id field is the document's primary key.

Indexing more than one field

In MongoDB, we can create an index that holds values for more than one field. We should call this kind of index a compound index. There is no big difference between a single field index and a compound index. The biggest difference is in the sort order. Before we move on to the particularities of compound indexes, let's use the customers collection to create our first compound index:

```
{
    "_id" : ObjectId("54aecd26867124b88608b4c9"),
    "username" : "customer1",
    "email" : "customer1@customer.com",
    "password" : "b1c5098d0c6074db325b0b9dddb068e1",
    "age" : 25,
    "address" : {
        "street" : "Street 1",
        "zipcode" : "87654321",
        "state" : "RJ"
    }
}
```

We can imagine that an application that wants to authenticate a customer uses the username and password fields together in a query like this:

```
db.customers.find(
{
username: "customer1",
password: "b1c5098d0c6074db325b0b9dddb068e1"
}
)
```

To enable better performance when executing this query, we can create an index of both the `username` and `password` fields:

```
db.customers.createIndex({username: 1, password: 1})
```

Nevertheless, for the following queries, does MongoDB use the compound index?

```
#Query 1
db.customers.find({username: "customer1"})
#Query 2
db.customers.find({password: "b1c5098d0c6074db325b0b9dddb068e1"})
#Query 3
db.customers.find(
{
    password: "b1c5098d0c6074db325b0b9dddb068e1",
    username: "customer1"
}
)
```

The answer is yes for `Query 1` and `Query 3`. As mentioned before, the order is very important in the creation of a compound index. The index created will have references to the documents sorted by the `username` field, and within each username entry, sorted by password entries. Thus, a query with only the `password` field as the criteria will not use the index.

Let's assume for a moment that we have the following index in the `customers` collection:

```
db.customers.createIndex(
{
    "address.state":1,
    "address.zipcode": 1,
    "address.street": 1
})
```

You might be asking which queries will use our new compound index? Before answering that question, we need to understand a compound index concept in MongoDB: the **prefix**. The prefix in a compound index is a subset of the indexed fields. As its name suggests, it is the fields that take precedence over other fields in the index. In our example, both `{"address.state":1}` and `{"address.state":1, "address.zipcode": 1}` are index prefixes.

A query that has any index prefix will use the compound index. Therefore, we can deduce that:

- Queries that include the `address.state` field will use the compound index
- Queries that include both the `address.state` and `address.zipcode` fields will also use the compound index
- Queries with `address.state`, `address.zipcode` and `address.street` will also use the compound index
- Queries with both `address.state` and `address.street` will also use the compound index

The compound index will not be used on queries that:

- Have only the `address.zipcode` field
- Have only the `address.street` field
- Have both the `address.zipcode` and `address.street` fields

 We should notice that, despite a query that has both `address.state` and `address.street` fields using the index, we could achieve a better performance in this query if we have single indexes for each field. This is explained by the fact that the compound index will be first sorted by `address.state`, followed by a sort on the `address.zipcode` field, and finally a sort on the `address.street` field. Thus, it is much more expensive for MongoDB to inspect this index than to inspect the other two indexes individually.

So, for this query:

```
db.customers.find(
{
    "address.state": "RJ",
    "address.street": "Street 1"
}
)
```

It would be more efficient if we have this index:

```
db.customers.createIndex({"address.state": 1, "address.street": 1})
```

Indexing multikey fields

Another way to create indexes in MongoDB is to create an index of an array field. These indexes can hold arrays of primitive values, such as strings and numbers, or even arrays of documents.

We must be particularly attentive while creating multikey indexes. Especially when we want to create a compound multikey index. It is not possible to create a compound index of two array fields.

 The main reason why we could not create an index of parallel arrays is because they will require the index to include an entry in the Cartesian product of the compound keys, which will result in a large index.

Consider the `customers` collection with documents like this one:

```
{
    "_id" : ObjectId("54aecd26867124b88608b4c9"),
    "username" : "customer1",
    "email" : "customer1@customer.com",
    "password" : "b1c5098d0c6074db325b0b9dddb068e1",
    "age" : 25,
    "address" : {
        "street" : "Street 1",
        "zipcode" : "87654321",
        "state" : "RJ"
    },
    "followedSellers" : [
        "seller1",
        "seller2",
        "seller3"
    ],
    "wishList" : [
        {
            "sku" : 123,
            "seller" : "seller1"
        },
        {
```

```
            "sku" : 456,
            "seller" : "seller2"
        },
        {
            "sku" : 678,
            "seller" : "seller3"
        }
    ]
}
```

We can create the following indexes for this collection:

```
db.customers.createIndex({followedSellers: 1})
```

```
db.customers.createIndex({wishList: 1})
```

```
db.customers.createIndex({"wishList.sku": 1})
```

```
db.customers.createIndex({"wishList.seller": 1})
```

But the following index cannot be created:

```
db.customers.createIndex({followedSellers: 1, wishList: 1}
```

Indexing for text search

Since its 2.4 version, MongoDB gives us the chance to create indexes that will help us in a text search. Although there are a wide variety of specialized tools for this, such Apache Solr, Sphinx, and ElasticSearch, most of the relational and NoSQL databases have full text searching natively.

It is possible to create a text index of a string or an array of string fields in a collection. For the following examples, we will use the products collection that we also used in *Chapter 3, Querying Documents*, but with some modification:

```
{
    "_id" : ObjectId("54837b61f059b08503e200db"),
    "name" : "Product 1",
    "description" :
    "Product 1 description",
    "price" : 10,
```

```
    "supplier" : {
        "name" : "Supplier 1",
        "telephone" : "+552199998888"
    },
    "review" : [
    {
        "customer" : {
            "email" : "customer@customer.com"
        },
        "stars" : 5
    }
    ],
    "keywords" : [ "keyword1", "keyword2", "keyword3" ]
}
```

We can create a text index just by specifying the `text` parameter in the `createIndex` method:

```
db.products.createIndex({name: "text"})
```

```
db.products.createIndex({description: "text"})
```

```
db.products.createIndex({keywords: "text"})
```

All the preceding commands could create a text index of the `products` collection. But, MongoDB has a limitation, in that we can only have one text index per collection. Thus, only one of the previous commands could be executed for the `products` collection.

Despite the limitation to create only one text index per collection, it is possible to create a compound text index:

```
db.products.createIndex({name: "text", description: "text"})
```

The preceding command creates a `text` index field for the `name` and `description` fields.

A common and useful way of creating a text index of a collection is to create an index for all text fields of the collection. There is a special syntax for creating this index, which you can see as follows:

```
db.products.createIndex({"$**","text"})
```

For a query to use a text index, we should use the `$text` operator in it. And, to better understand how to create an effective query, it is good to know how the indexes are created. As a matter of fact, the same process is used to execute the query using the `$text` operator.

To sum up the process, we can split it into three phases:

- Tokenization
- Removal of suffix and/or prefix, or stemming
- Removal of stop words

In order to optimize our queries, we can specify the language we are using in our text fields, and consequently in our text index, so that MongoDB will use a list of words in all three phases of the indexing process.

Since its 2.6 version, MongoDB supports the following languages:

- da **or** `danish`
- nl **or** `dutch`
- en **or** `english`
- fi **or** `finnish`
- fr **or** `french`
- de **or** `german`
- hu **or** `hungarian`
- it **or** `italian`
- nb **or** `norwegian`
- pt **or** `portuguese`
- ro **or** `romanian`
- ru **or** `russian`
- es **or** `spanish`
- sv **or** `swedish`
- tr **or** `turkish`

An example of an index creation with language could be:

```
db.products.createIndex({name: "text"},{ default_language: "pt"})
```

We can also opt to not use any language, by just creating the index with a none value:

```
db.products.createIndex({name: "text"},{ default_language: "none"})
```

By using the none value option, MongoDB will simply perform tokenization and stemming; it will not load any stop words list.

When we decide to use a text index, we should always double our attention. Every single detail will have a side effect on the way we design our documents. In previous versions of MongoDB, before creating a text index, we should change the allocation method for all collections to **usePowerOf2Sizes**. This is because text indexes are considered larger indexes.

Another major concern occurs at the moment we create the index. Depending on the size of the existing collection, the index could be very large, and to create a very large index we will need a lot of time. Thus, it is better to schedule this process to take place at a more timely opportunity.

Finally, we have to predict the impact that the text indexes will have on our write operations. This happens because, for each new record created in our collection, there will also be an entry created in the index referencing all the indexed value fields.

Creating special indexes

In addition to all the indexes types we've created until now, whether in ascending or descending order, or text typed, we have three more special indexes: time to live, unique, and sparse.

Time to live indexes

The **time to live** (TTL) index is an index based on lifetime. This index is created only in fields that are from the Date type. They cannot be compound and they will be automatically removed from the document after a given period of time.

This type of index can be created from a date vector. The document will expire at the moment when the lower array value is reached. MongoDB is responsible for controlling the documents' expiration through a background task at intervals of 60 seconds. For an example, let's use the `customers` collection we have been using in this chapter:

```
{
"_id" : ObjectId("5498da405d0ffdd8a07a87ba"),
"username" : "customer1",
"email" : "customer1@customer.com",
"password" : "b1c5098d0c6074db325b0b9dddb068e1",
"accountConfirmationExpireAt" : ISODate("2015-01-11T20:27:02.138Z")
}
```

The creation command that is based on the time to live index for the `accountConfirmationExpireAt` field will be the following:

```
db.customers.createIndex(
{accountConfirmationExpireAt: 1}, {expireAfterSeconds: 3600}
)
```

This command indicates that every document that is older than the value in seconds requested in the `expireAfterSeconds` field will be deleted.

There is also another way to create indexes based on lifetime, which is the scheduled way. The following example shows us this method of implementation:

```
db.customers.createIndex({
accountConfirmationExpireAt: 1}, {expireAfterSeconds: 0}
)
```

This will make sure that the document you saw in the previous example expires on January 11 2015, 20:27:02.

This type of index is very useful for applications that use machine-generated events, logs and session information, which need to be persistent only during a given period of time, as you will see once again in *Chapter 8, Logging and Real-time Analytics with MongoDB*.

Unique indexes

As with the vast majority of relational databases, MongoDB has a unique index. The unique index is responsible for rejecting duplicated values in the indexed field. The unique index can be created from a single or from a multikey field and as a compound index. When creating a unique compound index, there must be uniqueness in the values' combinations.

The default value for a unique field will always be null if we don't set any value during the `insert` operation. As you have seen before, the index created for the `_id` field of a collection is unique. Considering the last example of the `customers` collection, it's possible to create a unique index by executing the following:

```
db.customers.createIndex({username: 1}, {unique: true})
```

This command will create an index of the `username` field that will not allow duplicated values.

Sparse indexes

Sparse indexes are indexes that will be created only when the document has a value for the field that will be indexed. We can create sparse indexes using only one field from the document or using more fields. This last use is called a **compound index**. When we create compound indexes, it is mandatory that at least one of the fields has a not-null-value.

Take as an example the following documents in the `customers` collection:

```
{ "_id" : ObjectId("54b2e184bc471cf3f4c0a314"), "username" :
"customer1", "email" : "customer1@customer.com", "password" :
"b1c5098d0c6074db325b0b9dddb068e1" }

{ "_id" : ObjectId("54b2e618bc471cf3f4c0a316"), "username" :
"customer2", "email" : "customer2@customer.com", "password" :
"9f6a4a5540b8ebdd3bec8a8d23efe6bb" }

{ "_id" : ObjectId("54b2e629bc471cf3f4c0a317"), "username" : "customer3",
"email" : "customer3@customer.com" }
```

Using the following example command, we can create a `sparse` index in the `customers` collection:

```
db.customers.createIndex({password: 1}, {sparse: true})
```

The following example query uses the created index:

```
db.customers.find({password: "9f6a4a5540b8ebdd3bec8a8d23efe6bb"})
```

On the other hand, the following example query, which requests the descending order by the indexed field, will not use the index:

```
db.customers.find().sort({password: -1})
```

Summary

In this chapter, we looked at how indexes are a very important tool in the maintenance of a data model. By including index creation during the query planning stage, this will bring lot of benefits—most of all in what is referred to as performance during query documents.

Thus, you learned how to create a single, compound, and multikey indexes. Next, we covered how and when to use indexes for text searching on MongoDB. We then met special index types such as the TTL, unique, and sparse index.

In the next chapter, you will see how to analyze queries and consequently create them in a more efficient way.

5
Optimizing Queries

Now that we have taken a great step forward in comprehending how to improve read and write performance using indexes, let's see how we can analyze them if these indexes are behaving as expected, and also how indexes can influence a database's lifecycle. In addition to this, through this analysis, we will be able to evaluate and optimize the created queries and indexes.

So, in this chapter, we will study the concept of query plans and how MongoDB handles it. This includes understanding query covering and query selectivity, and how these plans behave when used in sharded environments and through replica sets.

Understanding the query plan

When we run a query, MongoDB will internally figure out the best way to do it by choosing from a set of possibilities extracted after query analysis (performed by the MongoDB query optimizer). These possibilities are called **query plans**.

To get a better understanding of a query plan, we must go back to the cursor concept and one of the cursor methods: explain(). The explain() method is one of the big changes in the MongoDB 3.0 release. It has been significantly enhanced due to the new query introspection system.

Not only has the output changed, as we saw earlier, but also the way we use it. We now can pass to the explain() method an option parameter that specifies the verbosity of the explain output. The possible modes are "queryPlanner", "executionStats", and "allPlansExecution". The default mode is "queryPlanner".

- In the "queryPlanner" mode, MongoDB runs the query optimizer to choose the winning plan under evaluation, and returns the information to the evaluated method.

- In the `"executionStats"` mode, MongoDB runs the query optimizer to choose the winning plan, executes it, and returns the information to the evaluated method. If we are executing the `explain()` method for a write operation, it returns the information about the operation that would be performed but does not actually execute it.

- Finally, in the `"allPlansExecution"` mode, MongoDB runs the query optimizer to choose the winning plan, executes it, and returns the information to the evaluated method as well as information for the other candidate plans.

> You can find more about the `explain()` method in the MongoDB 3.0 reference guide at `http://docs.mongodb.org/manual/reference/method/db.collection.explain/#db.collection.explain`.

The output of an `explain` execution shows us the query plans as a tree of stages. From the leaf to the root, each stage passes its results to the parent node. The first stage, which happens on the leaf node, accesses the collection or indices and passes the results to internal nodes. These internal nodes manipulate the results from which the final stage or the root node derives the result set.

There are four stages:

- `COLLSCAN`: This means that a full collection scan happened during this stage
- `IXSCAN`: This indicates that an index key scan happened during this stage
- `FETCH`: This is the stage when we are retrieving documents
- `SHARD_MERGE`: This is the stage where results that came from each shard are merged and passed to the parent stage

Detailed information about the winning plan stages can be found in the `explain.queryPlanner.winningPlan` key of the `explain()` execution output. The `explain.queryPlanner.winningPlan.stage` key shows us the name of the root stage. If there are one or more child stages, the stage will have an `inputStage` or `inputStages` key depending on how many stages we have. The child stages will be represented by the keys `explain.queryPlanner.winningPlan.inputStage` and `explain.queryPlanner.winningPlan.inputStages` of the `explain()` execution output.

> To learn more about the `explain()` method, visit the MongoDB 3.0 manual page at `http://docs.mongodb.org/manual/reference/explain-results/`.

All these changes in the execution and the output of the `explain()` method were made mainly to improve the DBAs' productivity. One of the biggest advantages compared to the previous MongoDB versions is that `explain()` does not need to execute the query to calculate the query plan. It also exposes query introspection to a wider range of operations including find, count, update, remove, group, and aggregate, giving DBAs the power to optimize queries of each type.

Evaluating queries

Getting straight to the point, the `explain` method will give us statistics from the query execution. For instance, we will see in these statistics whether a cursor is used or an index.

Let's use the following `products` collection as an example:

```
{
    "_id": ObjectId("54bee5c49a5bc523007bb779"),
    "name": "Product 1",
    "price": 56
}
{
    "_id": ObjectId("54bee5c49a5bc523007bb77a"),
    "name": "Product 2",
    "price": 64
}
{
    "_id": ObjectId("54bee5c49a5bc523007bb77b"),
    "name": "Product 3",
    "price": 53
}
{
    "_id": ObjectId("54bee5c49a5bc523007bb77c"),
    "name": "Product 4",
    "price": 50
}
{
    "_id": ObjectId("54bee5c49a5bc523007bb77d"),
    "name": "Product 5",
    "price": 89
```

```
}
{

    "_id": ObjectId("54bee5c49a5bc523007bb77e"),

    "name": "Product 6",

    "price": 69
}
{

    "_id": ObjectId("54bee5c49a5bc523007bb77f"),

    "name": "Product 7",

    "price": 71
}
{

    "_id": ObjectId("54bee5c49a5bc523007bb780"),

    "name": "Product 8",

    "price": 40
}
{

    "_id": ObjectId("54bee5c49a5bc523007bb781"),

    "name": "Product 9",

    "price": 41
}
{

    "_id": ObjectId("54bee5c49a5bc523007bb782"),

    "name": "Product 10",

    "price": 53
}
```

As we have already seen, when the collection is created, an index in the _id field is added automatically. To get all the documents in the collection, we will execute the following query in the mongod shell:

```
db.products.find({price: {$gt: 65}})
```

The result of the query will be the following:

```
{

    "_id": ObjectId("54bee5c49a5bc523007bb77d"),

    "name": "Product 5",

    "price": 89
```

```
}
{
    "_id": ObjectId("54bee5c49a5bc523007bb77e"),
    "name": "Product 6",
    "price": 69
}
{
    "_id": ObjectId("54bee5c49a5bc523007bb77f"),
    "name": "Product 7",
    "price": 71
}
```

To help you understand how MongoDB reaches this result, let's use the `explain` method on the cursor that was returned by the command `find`:

```
db.products.find({price: {$gt: 65}}).explain("executionStats")
```

The result of this operation is a document with information about the selected query plan:

```
{
    "queryPlanner" : {
        "plannerVersion" : 1,
        "namespace" : "ecommerce.products",
        "indexFilterSet" : false,
        "parsedQuery" : {
            "price" : {
                "$gt" : 65
            }
        },
        "winningPlan" : {
            "stage" : "COLLSCAN",
            "filter" : {
                "price" : {
                    "$gt" : 65
                }
            },
            "direction" : "forward"
        },
```

```
            "rejectedPlans" : [ ]
    },
    "executionStats" : {
        "executionSuccess" : true,
        "nReturned" : 3,
        "executionTimeMillis" : 0,
        "totalKeysExamined" : 0,
        "totalDocsExamined" : 10,
        "executionStages" : {
            "stage" : "COLLSCAN",
            "filter" : {
                "price" : {
                    "$gt" : 65
                }
            },
            "nReturned" : 3,
            "executionTimeMillisEstimate" : 0,
            "works" : 12,
            "advanced" : 3,
            "needTime" : 8,
            "needFetch" : 0,
            "saveState" : 0,
            "restoreState" : 0,
            "isEOF" : 1,
            "invalidates" : 0,
            "direction" : "forward",
            "docsExamined" : 10
        }
    },
    "serverInfo" : {
        "host" : "c516b8098f92",
        "port" : 27017,
        "version" : "3.0.2",
        "gitVersion" : "6201872043ecbbc0a4cc169b5482dcf385fc464f"
    },
    "ok" : 1
}
```

Initially, let's check only four fields in this document: queryPlanner.winningPlan.
stage, queryPlanner.executionStats.nReturned, queryPlanner.
executionStats.totalKeysExamined, and queryPlanner.executionStats.
totalDocsExamined:

- The queryPlanner.winningPlan.stage field is showing us that a full collection scan will be performed.

- The queryPlanner.executionStats.nReturned field shows how many documents match the query criteria. In other words, it shows us how many documents will be returned from the query execution. In this case, the result will be three documents.

- The queryPlanner.executionStats.totalDocsExamined field is the number of documents from the collection that will be scanned. In the example, all the documents were scanned.

- The queryPlanner.executionStats.totalKeysExamined field shows the number of index entries that were scanned.

- When executing a collection scan, as in the preceding example, nscanned also represents the number of documents scanned in the collection.

What happens if we create an index of the price field of our collection? Let's see:

```
db.products.createIndex({price: 1})
```

Obviously, the query result will be the same three documents that were returned in the previous execution. However, the result for the explain command will be the following:

```
{
    "queryPlanner" : {
        "plannerVersion" : 1,
        "namespace" : "ecommerce.products",
        "indexFilterSet" : false,
        "parsedQuery" : {
            ...
        },
        "winningPlan" : {
            "stage" : "FETCH",
            "inputStage" : {
                "stage" : "IXSCAN",
                "keyPattern" : {
                    "price" : 1
```

```
            },
            "indexName" : "price_1",
            ...
         }
      },
      "rejectedPlans" : [ ]
   },
   "executionStats" : {
      "executionSuccess" : true,
      "nReturned" : 3,
      "executionTimeMillis" : 20,
      "totalKeysExamined" : 3,
      "totalDocsExamined" : 3,
      "executionStages" : {
         "stage" : "FETCH",
         "nReturned" : 3,
         ...
         "inputStage" : {
            "stage" : "IXSCAN",
            "nReturned" : 3,
            ...
         }
      }
   },
   "serverInfo" : {
      ...
   },
   "ok" : 1
}
```

The returned document is fairly different from the previous one. Once again, let's focus on these four fields: `queryPlanner.winningPlan.stage`, `queryPlanner.executionStats.nReturned`, `queryPlanner.executionStats.totalKeysExamined`, and `queryPlanner.executionStats.totalDocsExamined`.

This time, we can see that we did not have a full collection scan. Instead of this, we had a FETCH stage with a child IXSCAN stage, as we can see in the queryPlanner.winningPlan.inputStage.stage field. This means that the query used an index. The name of the index can be found in the field queryPlanner.winningPlan.inputStage.indexName, in the example, price_1.

Furthermore, the mean difference in this result is that both queryPlanner.executionStats.totalDocsExamined and queryPlanner.executionStats.totalKeysExamined, returned the value 3, showing us that three documents were scanned. It is quite different from the 10 documents that we saw when executing the query without an index.

One point we should make is that the number of documents and keys scanned is the same as we can see in queryPlanner.executionStats.totalDocsExamined and queryPlanner.executionStats.totalKeysExamined. This means that our query was not covered by the index. In the next section, we will see how to cover a query using an index and what its benefits are.

Covering a query

Sometimes we can choose to create indexes with one or more fields, considering the frequency that they appear in our queries. We can also choose to create indexes in order to improve query performance, using them not only to match the criteria but also to extract results from the index itself.

We may say that, when we have a query, all the fields in the criteria are part of an index and when all the fields in the query are part of the same index, this query is covered by the index.

In the example shown in the previous section, we had an index created of the price field of the products collection:

```
db.products.createIndex({price: 1})
```

When we execute the following query, which retrieves the documents where the price field has a value greater than 65 but with a projection where we excluded the _id field from the result and included only the price field, we will have a different result from the one previously shown:

```
db.products.find({price: {$gt: 65}}, {price: 1, _id: 0})
```

The result will be:

```
{ "price" : 69 }
{ "price" : 71 }
{ "price" : 89 }
```

Then we analyze the query using the explain command, as follows:

```
db.products.explain("executionStats")
.find({price: {$gt: 65}}, {price: 1, _id: 0})
```

By doing this, we also have a different result from the previous example:

```
{
    "queryPlanner" : {
        "plannerVersion" : 1,
        "namespace" : "ecommerce.products",
        "indexFilterSet" : false,
        "parsedQuery" : {
            "price" : {
                "$gt" : 65
            }
        },
        "winningPlan" : {
            "stage" : "PROJECTION",
            . . .
            "inputStage" : {
                "stage" : "IXSCAN",
                . . .

            }
        },
        "rejectedPlans" : [ ]
    },
    "executionStats" : {
        "executionSuccess" : true,
        "nReturned" : 3,
        "executionTimeMillis" : 0,
        "totalKeysExamined" : 3,
        "totalDocsExamined" : 0,
        "executionStages" : {
            . . .
        }
    },
```

```
"serverInfo" : {
    ...
},
"ok" : 1
}
```

The first thing we notice is that the value of `queryPlanner.executionStats.totalDocsExamined` is `0`. This can be explained because our query is covered by the index. This means that we do not need to scan the documents from the collection. We will use the index to return the results, as we can observe in the value `3` for the `queryPlanner.executionStats.totalKeysExamined` field.

Another difference is that the `IXSCAN` stage is not a child of the `FETCH` stage. Every time that an index covers a query, `IXSCAN` will not be a descendent of the `FETCH` stage.

> Queries that are covered by the index can be extremely fast. This happens because the index keys are usually much smaller than the document itself and also because the index is in volatile memory or in disk sequential write mode.

Unfortunately, it's not always the case that we will have a query covered, even though we had the same conditions that were described previously.

Considering the following `customers` collection:

```
{
    "_id": ObjectId("54bf0d719a5bc523007bb78f"),
    "username": "customer1",
    "email": "customer1@customer.com",
    "password": "1185031ff57bfdaae7812dd705383c74",
    "followedSellers": [
        "seller3",
        "seller1"
    ]
}
{
    "_id": ObjectId("54bf0d719a5bc523007bb790"),
    "username": "customer2",
    "email": "customer2@customer.com",
```

```
      "password": "6362e1832398e7d8e83d3582a3b0c1ef",
      "followedSellers": [
         "seller2",
         "seller4"
      ]
   }
   {
      "_id": ObjectId("54bf0d719a5bc523007bb791"),
      "username": "customer3",
      "email": "customer3@customer.com",
      "password": "f2394e387b49e2fdda1b4c8a6c58ae4b",
      "followedSellers": [
         "seller2",
         "seller4"
      ]
   }
   {
      "_id": ObjectId("54bf0d719a5bc523007bb792"),
      "username": "customer4",
      "email": "customer4@customer.com",
      "password": "10619c6751a0169653355bb92119822a",
      "followedSellers": [
         "seller1",
         "seller2"
      ]
   }
   {
      "_id": ObjectId("54bf0d719a5bc523007bb793"),
      "username": "customer5",
      "email": "customer5@customer.com",
      "password": "30c25cf1d31cbccbd2d7f2100ffbc6b5",
      "followedSellers": [
         "seller2",
         "seller4"
      ]
   }
```

And an index created of the `followedSellers` field, executing the following command on mongod shell:

```
db.customers.createIndex({followedSellers: 1})
```

If we execute the following query on mongod shell, which was supposed to be covered by the index, since we are using `followedSellers` on the query criteria:

```
db.customers.find(
{
    followedSellers: {
        $in : ["seller1", "seller3"]
    }
},
{followedSellers: 1, _id: 0}
)
```

When we analyze this query using the `explain` command on the mongod shell, to see if the query is covered by the index, we can observe:

```
db.customers.explain("executionStats").find(
{
    followedSellers: {
        $in : ["seller1", "seller3"]
    }
},
{followedSellers: 1, _id: 0}
)
```

We have the following document as a result. We can see that, despite using a field that is in the index in the criteria and restricting the result to this field, the returned output has the FETCH stage as a parent of the IXSCAN stage. In addition, the values for `totalDocsExamined` and `totalKeysExamined` are different:

```
{
    "queryPlanner" : {
        "plannerVersion" : 1,
        "namespace" : "ecommerce.customers",
        ...
        "winningPlan" : {
            "stage" : "PROJECTION",
            ...
            "inputStage" : {
                "stage" : "FETCH",
```

```
            "inputStage" : {
                "stage" : "IXSCAN",
                "keyPattern" : {
                    "followedSellers" : 1
                },
                "indexName" : "followedSellers_1",
                ...
            }
        }
    },
    "rejectedPlans" : [ ]
},
"executionStats" : {
    "executionSuccess" : true,
    "nReturned" : 2,
    "executionTimeMillis" : 0,
    "totalKeysExamined" : 4,
    "totalDocsExamined" : 2,
    "executionStages" : {
        ...
    }
},
"serverInfo" : {
    ...
}
},
    "ok" : 1
}
```

The `totalDocsExamined` field returned 2, which means that it was necessary to scan two of the five documents from the collection. Meanwhile, the `totalKeysExamined` field returned 4, showing that it was necessary to scan four index entries for the returned result.

Another situation in which we do not have the query covered by an index is when the query execution is used in an index of a field that is part of an embedded document.

Let's check the example using the `products` collection that was already used in *Chapter 4, Indexing*, with an index of the `supplier.name` field:

```
db.products.createIndex({"supplier.name": 1})
```

The following query will not be covered by the index:

```
db.products.find(
    {"supplier.name": "Supplier 1"},
    {"supplier.name": 1, _id: 0}
)
```

 Remember that, though this query is not covered by the index, it will use the index in its plan.

Finally, when we are executing a query in a sharded collection, through **mongos**, this query will never be covered by an index.

The query optimizer

Now that you understand both evaluating query performance using the `explain()` method and how to take advantage of an index by covering a query, we will proceed to meet the huge responsibility of selecting and maintaining the query plan in MongoDB, the query optimizer.

The query optimizer is responsible for processing and selecting the best and most efficient query plan for a query. For this purpose, it takes into account all the collection indexes.

The process performed by the query optimizer is not an exact science, meaning that it is a little bit empirical—in other words, based on trial and error.

When we execute a query for the very first time, the query optimizer will run the query against all available indexes of the collection and choose the most efficient one. Thereafter, every time we run the same query or queries with the same pattern, the selected index will be used for the query plan.

Using the same `products` collection we used previously in this chapter, the following queries will run through the same query plan because they have the same pattern:

```
db.products.find({name: 'Product 1'})
db.products.find({name: 'Product 5'})
```

As the collection's data changes, the query optimizer re-evaluates it. Moreover, as the collection grows (more precisely for each 1,000 write operations, during each index creation, when the `mongod` process restarts, or when we call the `explain()` method), the optimizer re-evaluates itself.

Even with this marvelous automatic process known as the query optimizer, we may want to choose which index we want to use. For this, we use the `hint` method.

Suppose that we have these indexes in our previous `products` collection:

```
db.products.createIndex({name: 1, price: -1})
db.products.createIndex({price: -1})
```

If we want to retrieve all the products where the `price` field has a value greater than 10, sorted by the `name` field in descending order, use the following command to do this:

```
db.products.find({price: {$gt: 10}}).sort({name: -1})
```

The index chosen by the query optimizer will be the one created on the `name` and `price` fields, as we could see running the `explain()` method:

```
db.products.explain("executionStats").find({price: {$gt: 10}}).
sort({name: -1})
```

The result is:

```
{
    "queryPlanner" : {
        "plannerVersion" : 1,
        "namespace" : "ecommerce.products",
        ...
        "winningPlan" : {
            "stage" : "FETCH",
            ...
            "inputStage" : {
                "stage" : "IXSCAN",
                "keyPattern" : {
                    "name" : 1,
                    "price" : -1
                },
                "indexName" : "name_1_price_-1"
                ...
            }
        },
        ...
    },
```

```
   "executionStats" : {
      "executionSuccess" : true,
      "nReturned" : 10,
      "executionTimeMillis" : 0,
      "totalKeysExamined" : 10,
      "totalDocsExamined" : 10,
      "executionStages" : {
      ...
      }
   },
   "serverInfo" : {
      ...
   }
},
   "ok" : 1
}
```

However, we can force the use of the index only of the price field, in this manner:

```
db.products.find(
   {price: {$gt: 10}}
).sort({name: -1}).hint({price: -1})
```

To be certain, we use the explain method:

```
db.products.explain("executionStats").find(
   {price: {$gt: 10}}).sort({name: -1}
).hint({price: -1})
```

This produces the following document:

```
{
   "queryPlanner" : {
      "plannerVersion" : 1,
      "namespace" : "ecommerce.products",
      ...
      "winningPlan" : {
         "stage" : "SORT",
         ...
         "inputStage" : {
            "stage" : "KEEP_MUTATIONS",
```

```
            "inputStage" : {
                "stage" : "FETCH",
                "inputStage" : {
                    "stage" : "IXSCAN",
                    "keyPattern" : {
                        "price" : -1
                    },
                    "indexName" : "price_-1",
                    ...
                }
            }
        }
    },
    "rejectedPlans" : [ ]
},
"executionStats" : {
    "executionSuccess" : true,
    "nReturned" : 10,
    "executionTimeMillis" : 0,
    "totalKeysExamined" : 10,
    "totalDocsExamined" : 10,
    "executionStages" : {
        ...
    }
},
"serverInfo" : {
    ...
},
"ok" : 1
}
```

Reading from many MongoDB instances

So far, we have spoken a lot about reading from one MongoDB instance. Nevertheless, it is important that we speak briefly about reading from a sharded environment or from a replica set.

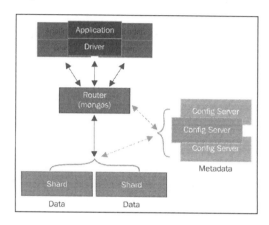

When we are reading from a shard, it is important to have the shard key as part of the query criteria. This is because, when we have the shard key, we will target the execution on one specific shard, whereas if we do not have the shard key, we will force the execution on all the shards in the cluster. Thus, the performance of a query in a sharded environment is linked to the shard key to a great extent.

By default, when we have a replica set in MongoDB, we will always read from the primary. We can modify this behavior to force a read operation execution on to a secondary node by modifying the read preferences.

Suppose that we have a replica set with three nodes: rs1s1, rs1s2, and rs1s3 and that rs1s1 is the primary node, and rs1s2 and rs1s3 are the secondary nodes. To execute a read operation forcing the read on a secondary node, we could do:

```
db.customers.find().readPref({mode: 'secondary'})
```

In addition, we have the following read preference options:

- `primary`, which is the default option and will force the user to read from the primary.

- `primaryPreferred`, which will read preferably from the primary but, in the case of unavailability, will read from a secondary.

- `secondaryPreferred`, which will read from a secondary but, in the case of unavailability, will read from the primary.

- `nearest`, which will read from the lowest network latency node in the cluster. In other words, with the shortest network distance, regardless of whether it is the primary or a secondary node.

In short, if our application wants to maximize consistency, then we should prioritize the read on the primary; when we are looking for availability, we should use `primaryPreferred` because we can guarantee consistency on most of the reads. When something goes wrong in the primary node, we can count on any secondary node. Finally, if we are looking for the lowest latency, we may use `nearest`, reminding ourselves that we do not have a guarantee of data consistency because we are prioritizing the lowest latency network node.

Summary

In this chapter, you learned to analyze query performance using MongoDB's native tools and to optimize our queries with this.

In the next chapter, we will talk about how to manage our database and its collections better by doing a functional or geographic segregation. You will also see how to maintain collections that should support a high read and write throughput.

6
Managing the Data

Planning a database operation is one of the most important phases of data model maintenance. In MongoDB, depending on the nature of the data, we can segregate the application's operations by functionality or by geographic groups.

In this chapter, we will review some concepts already introduced in *Chapter 5, Optimizing Queries*, such as read preferences and write concerns. But this time we will focus on understanding how these functionalities can help us to split the operations through MongoDB deployments, for instance, separating read and write operations, or ensuring information consistency using the write propagation through replica set nodes, considering the application's characteristics.

You will also see how it is possible to have collections that support a high read/write throughput—which is essential for some applications—by exploring special properties.

Therefore, in this chapter, you will learn about:

- Operational segregation
- Capped collections
- Data self-expiration

Operational segregation

So far, we have seen how our application's queries can influence, in general, our decisions regarding document design. However, there is more to the read preferences and write concern concepts than we have already explored.

MongoDB offers us a series of functionalities that allow us to segregate the application operations by functional or geographic groups. When using the functional segregation, we can direct an application responsible for report generation to use only a certain MongoDB deployment. The geographic segregation means that we can target operations considering the geographic distance from a MongoDB deployment.

Giving priority to read operations

It is not that hard to imagine that once an application is built, marketing or commercial people will ask for a new report of the application's data, and by the way, this will be the essential report. We know how dangerous it can be to build and plug such applications in our main database just for the purpose of reporting. Besides the data concurrence with other applications, we know that this type of application can overload our database by making complex queries and manipulating a huge amount of data.

This is the reason why we must target dedicated MongoDB deployments to the operations that handle huge volumes of data and need heavier processing from the database. We will make applications target the right MongoDB deployments through read preferences as you already saw in *Chapter 5, Optimizing Queries*.

By default, an application will always read the first node from our replica set. This behavior guarantees that the application will always read the most recent data, which ensures the data's consistency. Although, if the intention is to reduce the throughput in the first node, and we can accept eventual consistency, it is possible to redirect the read operations to secondary nodes from the replica set by enabling the `secondary` or `secondaryPreferred` mode.

Besides the function of throughput reduction on the primary node, giving preference to read operations in a secondary node is crucial when we have application distributed in multiple datacenters and consequently, we have replica sets distributed geographically. This is because we make it possible to choose the nearest node or a node with the lowest latency to execute the read operation by setting the nearest mode.

Finally, we can substantially increase the database's availability by allowing the read operations to be executed in any replica set node using the `primaryPreferred` mode.

But what if, in addition to the read preference specification, primary or secondary, we could specify in which instance we will target an operation? For instance, think of a replica set that is distributed in two different locations and each instance has a different type of physical storage. In addition to this, we want to ensure that the write operation will be performed in at least one instance of each datacenter that has an **ssd** disk. Is this possible? The answer is *yes*!

This is possible due to **tag sets**. Tags sets are a configuration property that give you control over write concerns and read preferences for a replica set. They consist of a document containing zero or more tags. We will store this configuration in the replica set configuration document in the `members[n].tags` field.

In the case of read preferences, the tag sets grant you target read operations for a specific member of a replica set. The tag sets values are applied when the replica set member for the read process is chosen.

The tag sets will affect only one of the read preference modes, which are `primaryPreferred`, `secondary`, `secondaryPreferred`, and `nearest`. The tag sets will have no effect on the `primary` mode, meaning that it will only impact the choice of a replica set secondary member, unless used in combination with the `nearest` mode, where the closest node or the less latency node can be the primary node.

Before we see how to do this configuration, you need to understand how the replica set member is chosen. The client driver that will perform the operation makes the choice, or in the case of a sharded cluster, the choice is done by the **mongos** instance.

Therefore, the choice process is done in the following way:

1. A list of the members, both primary and secondary, is created.
2. If a tag set is specified, the members that do not match the specification are skipped.
3. The client that is nearest to the application is determined.
4. A list of the other replica set members is created considering the latency among the other members. This latency can be defined as soon as the write operation is performed through the `secondaryAcceptableLatencyMS` property. In the case of a sharded cluster, it is set through the `--localThreshold` or `localPingThresholdMs` options. If none of these configurations are set, the default value will be 15 milliseconds.

You can find more about this configuration in the MongoDB manual reference at http://docs.mongodb.org/manual/reference/configuration-options/#replication. localPingThresholdMs.

5. The host that will be chosen to perform the operation is randomly selected and the read operation is performed.

The tag set configuration is as easy and simple as any other MongoDB configuration. As always, we use documents to create a configuration, and as stated before, the tag sets are a field of the replica set configuration document. This configuration document can be retrieved by running the conf() method on a replica set member.

You can find out more about the conf() method in the MongoDB documentation at http://docs.mongodb.org/manual/reference/method/rs.conf/#rs.conf.

The following document shows a tag set example for a read operation, after an execution of the rs.conf() command on the mongod shell of the rs1, which is our replica set's primary node:

```
rs1:PRIMARY> rs.conf()
{ // This is the replica set configuration document

    "_id" : "rs1",
    "version" : 4,
    "members" : [
        {
            "_id" : 0,
            "host" : "172.17.0.2:27017"
        },
        {
            "_id" : 1,
            "host" : "172.17.0.3:27017"
        },
        {
            "_id" : 2,
```

```
            "host" : "172.17.0.4:27017"
        }
    ]
}
```

To create a tag set configuration for each node of the replica set, we must do the following sequence of commands in the primary mongod shell:

First, we will get the replica set configuration document and store it in the cfg variable:

```
rs1:PRIMARY> cfg = rs.conf()
{
    "_id" : "rs1",
    "version" : 4,
    "members" : [
        {
            "_id" : 0,
            "host" : "172.17.0.7:27017"
        },
        {
            "_id" : 1,
            "host" : "172.17.0.5:27017"
        },
        {
            "_id" : 2,
            "host" : "172.17.0.6:27017"
        }
    ]
}
```

Then, by using the cfg variable, we will set a document as a new value to the members[n].tags field for each one of our three replica set members:

```
rs1:PRIMARY> cfg.members[0].tags = {"media": "ssd", "application":
"main"}
rs1:PRIMARY> cfg.members[1].tags = {"media": "ssd", "application":
"main"}
rs1:PRIMARY> cfg.members[2].tags = {"media": "ssd", "application":
"report"}
```

Finally, we call the `reconfig()` method, passing in our new configuration document stored in the `cfg` variable to reconfigure our replica set:

```
rs1:PRIMARY> rs.reconfig(cfg)
```

If everything is correct, then we must see this output in the mongod shell:

```
{ "ok" : 1 }
```

To check the configuration, we can re-execute the command `rs.conf()`. This will return the following:

```
rs1:PRIMARY> cfg = rs.conf()
{
    "_id" : "rs1",
    "version" : 5,
    "members" : [
        {
            "_id" : 0,
            "host" : "172.17.0.7:27017",
            "tags" : {
                "application" : "main",
                "media" : "ssd"
            }
        },
        {
            "_id" : 1,
            "host" : "172.17.0.5:27017",
            "tags" : {
                "application" : "main",
                "media" : "ssd"
            }
        },
        {
            "_id" : 2,
            "host" : "172.17.0.6:27017",
            "tags" : {
                "application" : "report",
```

```
            "media" : "ssd"
        }
    }
  ]
}
```

Now, consider the following customer collection:

```
{
    "_id": ObjectId("54bf0d719a5bc523007bb78f"),
    "username": "customer1",
    "email": "customer1@customer.com",
    "password": "1185031ff57bfdaae7812dd705383c74",
    "followedSellers": [
        "seller3",
        "seller1"
    ]
}
{
    "_id": ObjectId("54bf0d719a5bc523007bb790"),
    "username": "customer2",
    "email": "customer2@customer.com",
    "password": "6362e1832398e7d8e83d3582a3b0c1ef",
    "followedSellers": [
        "seller2",
        "seller4"
    ]
}
{
    "_id": ObjectId("54bf0d719a5bc523007bb791"),
    "username": "customer3",
    "email": "customer3@customer.com",
    "password": "f2394e387b49e2fdda1b4c8a6c58ae4b",
    "followedSellers": [
        "seller2",
        "seller4"
    ]
```

```
}
{

    "_id": ObjectId("54bf0d719a5bc523007bb792"),

    "username": "customer4",

    "email": "customer4@customer.com",

    "password": "10619c6751a0169653355bb92119822a",

    "followedSellers": [

        "seller1",

        "seller2"

    ]

}
{

    "_id": ObjectId("54bf0d719a5bc523007bb793"),

    "username": "customer5",

    "email": "customer5@customer.com",

    "password": "30c25cf1d31cbccbd2d7f2100ffbc6b5",

    "followedSellers": [

        "seller2",

        "seller4"

    ]

}
```

The following read operations will use the tags created in our replica set's instances:

```
db.customers.find(
    {username: "customer5"}
).readPref(
    {
        tags: [{application: "report", media: "ssd"}]
    }
)
db.customers.find(
    {username: "customer5"}
).readPref(
    {
        tags: [{application: "main", media: "ssd"}]
    }
)
```

The preceding configuration is an example of *segregation by application operation*. We created tag sets, marking the application's nature and what the media type that will be read will be.

As we have seen before, tag sets are very useful when we need to separate our application geographically. Suppose that we have MongoDB applications and instances of our replica set in two different datacenters. Let's create tags that will indicate in which datacenter our instances are present by running the following sequence on the replica set primary node mongod shell. First, we will get the replica set configuration document and store it in the `cfg` variable:

```
rs1:PRIMARY> cfg = rs.conf()
```

Then, by using the `cfg` variable, we will set a document as a new value to the `members[n].tags` field, for each one of our three replica set members:

```
rs1:PRIMARY> cfg.members[0].tags = {"media": "ssd", "application":
"main", "datacenter": "A"}
rs1:PRIMARY> cfg.members[1].tags = {"media": "ssd", "application":
"main", "datacenter": "B"}
rs1:PRIMARY> cfg.members[2].tags = {"media": "ssd", "application":
"report", "datacenter": "A"}
```

Finally, we call the `reconfig()` method, passing our new configuration document stored in the `cfg` variable to reconfigure our replica set:

```
rs1:PRIMARY> rs.reconfig(cfg)
```

If everything is correct, then we will see this output in the mongod shell:

```
{ "ok" : 1 }
```

The result of our configuration can be checked by executing the command `rs.conf()`:

```
rs1:PRIMARY> rs.conf()
{
    "_id" : "rs1",
    "version" : 6,
    "members" : [
        {
            "_id" : 0,
            "host" : "172.17.0.7:27017",
            "tags" : {
```

```
            "application" : "main",
            "datacenter" : "A",
            "media" : "ssd"
        }
    },
    {
        "_id" : 1,
        "host" : "172.17.0.5:27017",
        "tags" : {
            "application" : "main",
            "datacenter" : "B",
            "media" : "ssd"
        }
    },
    {
        "_id" : 2,
        "host" : "172.17.0.6:27017",
        "tags" : {
            "application" : "report",
            "datacenter" : "A",
            "media" : "ssd"
        }
    }
    ]
}
```

In order to target a read operation to a given datacenter, we must specify it in a new tag inside our query. The following queries will use the tags and each one will be executed in its own datacenter:

```
db.customers.find(
    {username: "customer5"}
).readPref(
    {tags: [{application: "main", media: "ssd", datacenter: "A"}]}
) // It will be executed in the replica set' instance 0
db.customers.find(
```

```
    {username: "customer5"}
).readPref(
    {tags: [{application: "report", media: "ssd", datacenter: "A"}]}
) //It will be executed in the replica set's instance 2
db.customers.find(
    {username: "customer5"}
).readPref(
    {tags: [{application: "main", media: "ssd", datacenter: "B"}]}
) //It will be executed in the replica set's instance 1
```

In write operations, the tag sets are not used to choose the replica set member that will be available to write. Although, it is possible to use tag sets in write operations through the creation of custom write concerns.

Let's get back to the requirement raised at the beginning of this section. How can we ensure that a write operation will be spread over at least two instances of a geographic area? By running the sequence of the following commands on the replica set primary node mongod shell, we will configure a replica set with five instances:

```
rs1:PRIMARY> cfg = rs.conf()
rs1:PRIMARY> cfg.members[0].tags = {"riodc": "rack1"}
rs1:PRIMARY> cfg.members[1].tags = {"riodc": "rack2"}
rs1:PRIMARY> cfg.members[2].tags = {"riodc": "rack3"}
rs1:PRIMARY> cfg.members[3].tags = {"spdc": "rack1"}
rs1:PRIMARY> cfg.members[4].tags = {"spdc": "rack2"}
rs1:PRIMARY> rs.reconfig(cfg)
```

The tags `riodc` and `spdc` represent which localities our instances are physically present in.

Now, let's create a custom `writeConcern` MultipleDC using the property `getLastErrorModes`. This will ensure that the write operation will be spread to at least one location member.

To do this, we will execute the preceding sequence, where we set a document representing our custom write concern on the `settings` field of our replica set configuration document:

```
rs1:PRIMARY> cfg = rs.conf()
rs1:PRIMARY> cfg.settings = {getLastErrorModes: {MultipleDC: {"riodc": 1,
"spdc":1}}}
```

The output in the mongod shell should look like this:

```
{
    "getLastErrorModes" : {
        "MultipleDC" : {
            "riodc" : 1,
            "spdc" : 1
        }
    }
}
```

Then we call the `reconfig()` method, passing the new configuration:

```
rs1:PRIMARY> rs.reconfig(cfg)
```

If the execution was successful, the output in the mongod shell is a document like this:

```
{ "ok" : 1 }
```

From this moment, we can use a `writeConcern` MultipleDC in order to ensure that the write operation will be performed in at least one node of each data center shown, as follows:

```
db.customers.insert(
    {
        username: "customer6",
        email: "customer6@customer.com",
        password: "1185031ff57bfdaae7812dd705383c74",
        followedSellers: ["seller1", "seller3"]
    },
    {
        writeConcern: {w: "MultipleDC"}
    }
)
```

Back to our requirement, if we want the write operation to be performed in at least two instances of each datacenter, we must configure it in the following way:

```
rs1:PRIMARY> cfg = rs.conf()
rs1:PRIMARY> cfg.settings = {getLastErrorModes: {MultipleDC: {"riodc": 2,
"spdc":2}}}
rs1:PRIMARY> rs.reconfig(cfg)
```

And, fulfilling our requirement, we can create a `writeConcern` MultipleDC called ssd. This will ensure that the write operation will happen in at least one instance that has this type of disk:

```
rs1:PRIMARY> cfg = rs.conf()
rs1:PRIMARY> cfg.members[0].tags = {"riodc": "rack1", "ssd": "ok"}
rs1:PRIMARY> cfg.members[3].tags = {"spdc": "rack1", "ssd": "ok"}
rs1:PRIMARY> rs.reconfig(cfg)
rs1:PRIMARY> cfg.settings = {getLastErrorModes: {MultipleDC: {"riodc": 2,
"spdc":2}, ssd: {"ssd": 1}}}
rs1:PRIMARY> rs.reconfig(cfg)
```

In the following query, we see how using a `writeConcern` MultipleDC requires the write operation to be present in at least one instance that has ssd:

```
db.customers.insert(
    {
        username: "customer6",
        email: "customer6@customer.com",
        password: "1185031ff57bfdaae7812dd705383c74",
        followedSellers: ["seller1", "seller3"]
    },
    {
        writeConcern: {w: "ssd"}
    }
)
```

It is not a simple task to make an operational segregation in our database. However, it is very useful for the database's management and maintenance. The early implementation of this kind of task requires a good knowledge of our data model, as details about the storage our database resides in are highly important.

In the next section, we will see how to plan collections for applications that need high throughput and fast response times.

 If you want to learn more about how to configure replica set tag sets, you can visit the MongoDB reference manual at http://docs. mongodb.org/manual/tutorial/configure-replica-set-tag-sets/#replica-set-configuration-tag-sets.

Capped collections

Non-functional requirements are often related to the application's response time. Especially nowadays when we are connected to news feeds all the time and we want fresh information to be available in the shortest response time.

MongoDB has a special type of collection that meets this non-functional requirement, capped collections. Capped collections are fixed size collections that support high read and write throughput. This is because the documents are inserted in their natural order, without the need for an index to perform the write operation.

The natural insertion order is guaranteed by MongoDB, which writes the data like it is written on the disk. Therefore, updates that increase the document size are not allowed during the document's lifecycle. As soon as the collection reaches maximum size, MongoDB automatically cleans old documents so that new documents can be inserted.

One very common use case is the persistence of application logs. MongoDB itself uses the replica set operation log, `oplog.rs`, as a capped collection. In *Chapter 8, Logging and Real-time Analytics with MongoDB*, you will see another practical example of this.

Another very common usage of MongoDB is as a publisher/subscriber system, especially if we use tailable cursors. Tailable cursors are cursors that remain open even after the client reads all the returned records. So, when new documents are inserted into the collection, the cursor returns it to the client.

The following command creates the `ordersQueue` collection:

```
db.createCollection("ordersQueue",{capped: true, size: 10000})
```

We used the `util` command `createCollection` to create our capped collection, passing to it the name `ordersQueue` and a collection with the `capped` property with the value `true` and `size` with a value of `10000`. If the `size` property is less than 4,096, MongoDB adjusts it to 4,096 bytes. On the other hand, if it is greater than 4,096, MongoDB raises the size and adjusts it to be a multiple of 256.

Optionally, we can set the maximum document number that a collection can have by using the `max` property:

```
db.createCollection(
    "ordersQueue",
    {capped: true, size: 10000, max: 5000}
)
```

If we need to convert a collection into a capped collection, we should use the `convertToCapped` method as follows:

```
db.runCommand(
    {"convertToCapped": " ordersQueue ", size: 100000}
)
```

As we have already seen, MongoDB keeps the documents in a natural order, in other words, the order in which they are inserted into MongoDB. Consider the following documents, inserted in the `ordersQueue` collection as shown:

```
{
    "_id" : ObjectId("54d97db16840a9a7c089fa30"),
    "orderId" : "order_1",
    "time" : 1423539633910
}
{
    "_id" : ObjectId("54d97db66840a9a7c089fa31"),
    "orderId" : "order_2",
    "time" : 1423539638006
}
{
    "_id" : ObjectId("54d97dba6840a9a7c089fa32"),
    "orderId" : "order_3",
    "time" : 1423539642022
}
{
    "_id" : ObjectId("54d97dbe6840a9a7c089fa33"),
    "orderId" : "order_4",
    "time" : 1423539646015
}
{
    "_id" : ObjectId("54d97dcf6840a9a7c089fa34"),
    "orderId" : "order_5",
    "time" : 1423539663559
}
```

The query db.ordersQueue.find() produces the following result:

```
{
    "_id" : ObjectId("54d97db16840a9a7c089fa30"),
    "orderId" : "order_1",
    "time" : 1423539633910
}
{
    "_id" : ObjectId("54d97db66840a9a7c089fa31"),
    "orderId" : "order_2",
    "time" : 1423539638006
}
{
    "_id" : ObjectId("54d97dba6840a9a7c089fa32"),
    "orderId" : "order_3",
    "time" : 1423539642022
}
{
    "_id" : ObjectId("54d97dbe6840a9a7c089fa33"),
    "orderId" : "order_4",
    "time" : 1423539646015
}
{
    "_id" : ObjectId("54d97dcf6840a9a7c089fa34"),
    "orderId" : "order_5",
    "time" : 1423539663559
}
```

If we use the $natural operator as shown in the following query, we will have the same result as shown in the preceding output:

```
db.ordersQueue.find().sort({$natural: 1})
```

But if we need the last insertion first, we must execute the command with a -1 value on the $natural operator:

```
db.ordersQueue.find().sort({$natural: -1})
```

We must be careful when creating a capped collection as:

- We cannot shard a capped collection.

- We cannot update a document in a capped collection; otherwise, the document grows in size. If we need to update a document in a capped collection, then we must make sure that the size will remain the same. And for better performance, we should create an index to avoid a collection scan when updating.

- We cannot delete a document in a capped collection.

Capped collections are a good tool when we have a high read/write throughput as a non-functional requirement, or we need to limit the collection size in bytes or by document number.

Nonetheless, if we need to automatically expire data, based on a time frame, we should use the **time to live** (**TTL**) function.

Data self-expiration

As you already saw in *Chapter 4, Indexing,* MongoDB offers us an index type that helps us to remove data from a collection after a certain amount of time in seconds, or by a specific date.

Indeed, the TTL is a background thread that executes on a mongod instance that looks for documents with date typed fields on the index, and removes them.

Consider a `customers` collection with the following document:

```
{
    "_id" : ObjectId("5498da405d0ffdd8a07a87ba"),
    "username" : "customer1",
    "email" : "customer1@customer.com",
    "password" : "b1c5098d0c6074db325b0b9dddb068e1",
    "accountConfirmationExpireAt" : ISODate
    ("2015-01-11T20:27:02.138Z")
}
```

To expire the documents in this collection after 360 seconds, we should create the following index:

```
db.customers.createIndex(
    {accountConfirmationExpireAt: 1},
    {expireAfterSeconds: 3600}
)
```

To expire the documents at exactly 2015-01-11 20:27:02, we should create the following index:

```
db.customers.createIndex(
    {accountConfirmationExpireAt: 1},
    {expireAfterSeconds: 0}
)
```

When using the TTL function, we must take extra care and keep the following points in mind:

- We cannot create a TTL index on a capped collection because MongoDB will not be able to remove documents from the collection.
- A TTL index cannot have a field that is part of another index.
- The field of the index should be a Date or array of a Date type.
- Despite having the background thread in every replica set node, which removes the documents when we have a TTL index, it will only remove them from the primary one. The replication process will delete the documents from the secondary nodes of the replica set.

Summary

In this chapter, you saw that besides thinking of our schema design based on our queries, it is also important to think about the planning of the operation and maintenance for the creation of our collections.

You learned how to use tag sets to deal with datacenter-aware operations and why we limit the amount of documents stored in our collections by doing a capped collection. In the same manner, you saw how TTL indexes can be useful in real-life use cases.

In the next chapter, you will see how we can scale our MongoDB instance by creating shards.

7
Scaling

Scalability has been a much-discussed subject over the years. Even though many things have already been said about it, this topic is very important and here, in this book, it will surely find its place too.

It is not in our interest to deal with all the concepts that involve database scalability, especially in NoSQL databases, but to show the possibilities that MongoDB offers when working with scalability in our collections and also how the flexibility of MongoDB's data model can influence our choices.

It is possible to horizontally scale MongoDB based on a simple infrastructure and low-cost sharding requests. Sharding is the technique of distributing data through multiple physical partitions called **shards**. Even though the database is physically partitioned, to our clients the database itself is a single instance. The technique of sharding is completely transparent for the database's clients.

Dear reader, get ready! In this chapter, you will see some crucial topics for database maintenance, such as:

- Scaling out with sharding
- Choosing the shard key
- Scaling a social inbox schema design

Scaling out MongoDB with sharding

When we talk about database scalability, we have two reference methods:

- **Scale up or vertical scale**: In this method, we add more resources to a machine. For example, a CPU, disk, and memory in order to increase the system's capacity.
- **Scale out or horizontal scale**: In this method, we add more nodes to the systems and distribute the work among the available nodes.

The choice between one or the other does not depend on our desire. It depends on the system that we want to scale. It is necessary to know whether it is possible to scale that system in the way that we want to. We must also keep in mind that there is a difference and trade-off between the two techniques.

Increasing the storage capacity, CPU, or memory can be very expensive and sometimes impossible due to our service provider's limitations. On the other hand, increasing the number of nodes in a system can also increase complexity both conceptually and operationally.

However, considering the advances in virtualization technology and the facilities offered by cloud providers, scaling horizontally is becoming the more practical solution for some applications.

MongoDB is prepared to scale horizontally. This is done with the help of a technique of sharding. This technique consists of partitioning our data set and distributing the data among many servers. The main purpose of sharding is to support bigger databases that are able to deal with a high-throughput operation by distributing the operation's load between each shard.

For example, if we have a 1-terabyte database and four configured shards, each shard should have 256 GB of data. But, this does not mean that each shard will manage 25 percent of throughput operation. This will only depend on the way that we decided to construct our shard. This is a big challenge and the main target of this chapter.

The following diagram demonstrates how a shard works on MongoDB:

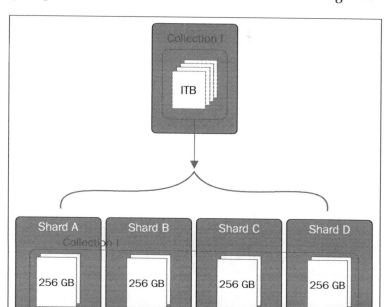

At the time that this book was written, MongoDB, in its 3.0 version, offers multiple sharding policies: **range-based**, **hash-based**, and **location-based** sharding.

- In the range-based policy, MongoDB will partition the data based on the value for the shard key. The documents that the shard key values close to each other will be allocated in the same shard.

- In the hash-based policy, the documents are distributed considering the MD5 value for the shard key.

- In the location-based policy, the documents will be distributed in shards based on a configuration that will associate shard range values with a specific shard. This configuration uses tags to do this, which is very similar to what you saw in *Chapter 6, Managing the Data*, where we discussed operation segregation.

Sharding works in MongoDB at the collections level, which means we can have collections with sharding and without sharding enabled in the same database. To set sharding in a collection, we must configure a sharded cluster. The elements for a sharded cluster are shards, query routers, and configuration servers:

- A **shard** is where a part of our data set will be allocated. A shard can be a MongoDB instance or a replica set

- The **query router** is the interface offered for the database clients that will be responsible for directing the operations to the correct shard

- The **config server** is a MongoDB instance that is responsible for keeping the sharded cluster configurations or, in other words, the cluster's metadata

The following diagram shows a shared cluster and its components:

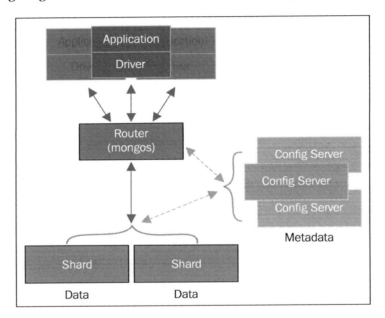

We will not go any deeper into the creation and maintenance of a sharded cluster, as this is not our objective in this chapter. However, it is important to know that the sharded cluster's setup depends on the scenario.

In a production environment, the minimum recommended setup is at least three configuration servers, two or more replica sets, which will be our shards, and one or more query routers. By doing this, we can ensure the minimum redundancy and high availability for our environment.

Choosing the shard key

Once we've decided that we have the need for a sharded cluster, the next step is to choose the shard key. The shard key is responsible for determining the distribution of documents among the cluster's shards. These will also be a key factor in determining the success or the failure of our database.

For each write operation, MongoDB will allocate a new document based on the range value for the shard key. A shard key's range is also known as a **chunk**. A chunk has a default length of 64 MB, but if you want this value to be customized to your need, it can be configured. In the following diagram, you can see how documents are distributed on chunks given an numeric shard key from infinity negative to infinity positive:

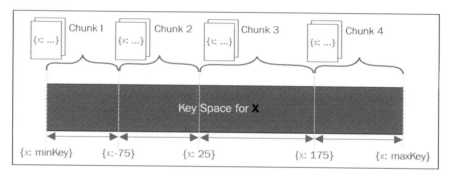

Before starting a discussion about the things that can affect our shard key's construction, there are some limitations in MongoDB that must be respected. These limitations are significant and, in some ways, they help us to eliminate the possibilities of some errors in our choices.

A shard key cannot exceed a length of 512 bytes. A shard key is an indexed field in the document. This index can be a simple field or a composed field, but it will never be a multikey field. It is also possible to use indexes of simple hash fields since the 2.4 version of MongoDB.

The following information must be read quietly, like a mantra, so you will not make any mistakes from the very beginning.

You have to keep one thing in your mind: the shard key is unchangeable.

To repeat, the shard key is unchangeable. That means, dear reader, that once a shard key is created, you can never change it. Never!

You can find detailed information about MongoDB sharded cluster limitations in the MongoDB manual reference at `http://docs.mongodb.org/manual/reference/limits/#sharded-clusters`.

But what if I created a shard key and I want to change it? What should I do? Instead of trying to change it, we should do the following:

1. Execute a dump of the database in a disk file.
2. Drop the collection.
3. Configure a new collection using the new shard key.
4. Execute a pre-split of the chunks.
5. Recover the dump file.

As you can see, we do not change the shard key. We recreated almost everything from scratch. Therefore, be careful when executing the command for shard key's creation or you will get a headache if you need to change it.

The next piece of information you need to remember is that you cannot update the value of one or more fields that are a part of the shard key. In other words, the value for a shard key is also unchangeable.

There is no use in trying to execute the `update()` method in a field that is part of a shard key. It will not work.

Before we proceed, let's see in practice what we discussed until this point. Let's create a sharded cluster for testing. The following shard configuration is very useful for testing and developing. Never use this configuration in a production environment. The commands given will create:

- Two shards
- One configuration server
- One query router

As a first step, let's start a configuration server instance. The configuration server is nothing more than a `mongod` instance with the initialization parameter `--configsvr`. If we do not set a value for the parameter `--port <port number>`, it will start on port 27019 by default:

```
mongod --fork --configsvr --dbpath /data/configdb --logpath /log/
configdb.log
```

The next step is to start the query router. The query router is a `mongos` MongoDB instance, which route queries and write operations to shards, using the parameter `--configdb <configdb hostname or ip:port>`, which indicates the configuration server. By default, MongoDB starts it on port 27017:

```
mongos --fork --configdb localhost --logpath /log/router.log
```

Finally, let's start the shards. The shards in this example will be just two simple instances of `mongod`. Similar to `mongos`, a `mongod` instance starts on port 27017 by default. As we already started the `mongos` instance on this port, let's set a different port for the `mongod` instance:

```
mongod --fork --dbpath /data/mongod1 --port 27001 --logpath /log/mongod1.
log
```

```
mongod --fork --dbpath /data/mongod2 --port 27002 --logpath /log/mongod2.
log
```

Done! Now we have the basic infrastructure for our test sharded cluster. But, wait! We do not have a sharded cluster yet. The next step is to add the shards to the cluster. To do this, we must connect the `mongos` instance that we already started to the query router:

```
mongo localhost:27017
```

Once on the `mongos` shell, we have to execute the `addShard` method in the following way:

```
mongos> sh.addShard("localhost:27001")
```

```
mongos> sh.addShard("localhost:27002")
```

If we want to check the result of the preceding operations, we can execute the `status()` command and see some information about the created shard:

```
mongos> sh.status()
--- Sharding Status ---
  sharding version: {
```

```
    "_id" : 1,
    "minCompatibleVersion" : 5,
    "currentVersion" : 6,
    "clusterId" : ObjectId("54d9dc74fadbfe60ef7b394e")
}
  shards:
    { "_id" : "shard0000", "host" : "localhost:27001" }
    { "_id" : "shard0001", "host" : "localhost:27002" }
  databases:
    { "_id" : "admin", "partitioned" : false, "primary" : "config" }
```

In the returned document, we can only see basic information, such as which the hosts are for our sharded cluster and the databases that we have. For now, we do not have any collection using the sharding enabled. For that reason, the information is greatly simplified.

Now that we have the shards, the configuration server, and the query router, let's enable sharding in the database. It is necessary first to enable sharding in a database before doing the same for a collection. The following command enables sharding in a database called ecommerce:

```
mongos> sh.enableSharding("ecommerce")
```

By consulting the sharded cluster's status, we can notice that we have information about our ecommerce database:

```
mongos> sh.status()
--- Sharding Status ---
  sharding version: {
    "_id" : 1,
    "minCompatibleVersion" : 5,
    "currentVersion" : 6,
    "clusterId" : ObjectId("54d9dc74fadbfe60ef7b394e")
}
  shards:
    { "_id" : "shard0000", "host" : "172.17.0.23:27017" }
    { "_id" : "shard0001", "host" : "172.17.0.24:27017" }
  databases:
```

```
{ "_id" : "admin", "partitioned" : false, "primary" : "config" }
{ "_id" : "ecommerce", "partitioned" : true, "primary" :
"shard0000" }
```

Consider that in the `ecommerce` database, we have a `customers` collection with the following documents:

```
{
    "_id" : ObjectId("54fb7110e7084a229a66eda2"),
    "isActive" : true,
    "age" : 28,
    "name" : "Paige Johnson",
    "gender" : "female",
    "email" : "paigejohnson@combot.com",
    "phone" : "+1 (830) 484-2397",
    "address" : {
        "city" : "Dennard",
        "state" : "Kansas",
        "zip" : 2492,
        "latitude" : -56.564242,
        "longitude" : -160.872178,
        "street" : "998 Boerum Place"
    },
    "registered" : ISODate("2013-10-14T14:44:34.853Z"),
    "friends" : [
        {
            "id" : 0,
            "name" : "Katelyn Barrett"
        },
        {
            "id" : 1,
            "name" : "Weeks Valentine"
        },
        {
            "id" : 2,
```

```
        "name"  :  "Wright Jensen"
    }
  ]
}
```

We must execute the `shardCollection` command to enable sharding in this collection, using the collection name and a document that will represent our shard key as a parameter.

Let's enable the shard in the `customers` collection by executing the following command in the `mongos` shell:

```
mongos> sh.shardCollection("ecommerce.customers", {"address.zip": 1,
"registered": 1})
{
    "proposedKey" : {
        "address.zip" : 1,
        "registered" : 1
    },
    "curIndexes" : [
        {
            "v" : 1,
            "key" : {
                "_id" : 1
            },
            "name" : "_id_",
            "ns" : "ecommerce.customers"
        }
    ],
    "ok" : 0,
    "errmsg" : "please create an index that starts with the shard key
before sharding."
}
```

As you can see, something went wrong during the command's execution. MongoDB is warning us that we must have an index and the shard key must be a prefix. So, we must execute the following sequence on the mongos shell:

```
mongos> db.customers.createIndex({"address.zip": 1, "registered": 1})
mongos> sh.shardCollection("ecommerce.customers", {"address.zip": 1, "registered": 1})
{ "collectionsharded" : "ecommerce.customers", "ok" : 1 }
```

Well done! Now we have the customers collection of the ecommerce database with the shard enabled.

 If you are sharding an empty collection, the shardCollection command will create the index of the shard key.

But what was the factor that determined the choice of address.zip and registered as the shard key? In this case, as I said before, I chose a random field just to illustrate. From now on, let's think about what factors can establish the creation of a good shard key.

Basic concerns when choosing a shard key

The choice of which shard key is not an easy task and there is no recipe for it. Most of the time, knowing our domain and its use in advance is fundamental. It is essential to be very careful when doing this. A not-so-appropriate shard key can bring us a series of problems in our database and consequently affect its performance.

First of all is divisibility. We must think of a shard key that allows us to visualize the documents' division among the shards. A shard key with a limited number of values may result in "unsplittable" chunks.

We can state that this field must have a high cardinality, such as fields with a high variety of values and also unique fields. Identifications fields such as e-mail addresses, usernames, phone numbers, social security numbers, and zip codes are a good example of fields with high cardinality.

In fact, each one of them can be unique if we take into account a certain situation. In an ecommerce system, if we have a document that is related to shipment, we will have more than one document with the same zip code. But, consider another example, a catalogue system for beauty salons in a city. Then, if a document represents a beauty salon, the zip code will be a more unique number than it was in the previous example.

The third is maybe the most polemical point until now because it contradicts the last one in a certain way. We have seen that a shard key with a high randomness degree is good practice in trying to increase the performance in write operations. Now, we will consider a shard key's creation to target a single shard. When we think about performance on read operations, it is a good idea to read from a single shard. As you already know, in a sharded cluster, the database complexity is abstracted on the query router. In other words, it is **mongos'** responsibility to discover which shards it should search for the information requested in a query. If our shard key is distributed across multiple shards, then mongos will search for the information on the shards, collect and merge them all, and then deliver it. But, if the shard key was planned to target a single shard, then the mongos task will search for the information in this unique shard and, in sequence, deliver it.

The fourth and last point is about cases when we do not have any field in the document that would be a good choice for our shard key. In this situation, we must think about a composed shard key. In the previous example, we use a composed shard key with the fields `address.zip` and `registered`. A composed shard key will also help us to have a more divisible key due the fact that if the first value from the shard key does not have a high cardinality, adding a second value will increase the cardinality.

So, these basic concerns show us that depending on what we want to search for, we should choose different approaches for the shard key's document. If we need query insulation, then a shard key that can focus on one shard is a good choice. But, when we need to escalate the write operation, the more random our shard key, the better it will be for performance.

Scaling a social inbox schema design

On October 31, 2014, MongoDB Inc. introduced on their community blog three different approaches to solve a very common problem, social inboxes.

 If you want to see the blog post, refer to `http://blog.mongodb.org/post/65612078649/schema-design-for-social-inboxes-in-mongodb`.

From the three presented schema designs, it is possible to see the application of all the scaling concepts we have seen until now in an easy and efficient way. In all of the cases, the concept of a fan out applies, in which the workload is distributed among the shards in parallel. Each approach has its own application according to the needs of the database client.

The three schema designs are:

- Fan out on read
- Fan out on write
- Fan out on write with buckets

Fan out on read

The fan out on read design bears this name due to the query router's behavior when a client reads an inbox. It is considered to be the design with the simplest mechanics compared to the others. It is also the easiest to implement.

In the fan out on read design, we will have one `inbox` collection, where we will insert every new message. The document that will reside on this collection has four fields:

- `from`: A string that represents the message sender
- `to`: An array with all message recipients
- `sent`: A date field that represents when the message was sent to the recipients
- `message`: A string field that represents the message itself

In the following document, we can see an example of a message sent from John to Mike and Billie:

```
{
from: "John",
to: ["Mike", "Billie"],
sent: new Date(),
message: "Hey Mike, Billie"
}
```

The operations on this collection will be the most straightforward of all. To send a message is to make an insert operation in the `inbox` collection, while to read is to find all the messages with a specific recipient.

The first thing to be done is to enable sharding on the database. Our `inbox` collection is in a database called `social`. To do this, and all other things that we will do in this chapter, we will use the `mongos` shell. So, let's start out:

```
mongos> sh.enableSharding("social")
```

Now, we will have to create the collection's shard key. To implement this design, we will create a shard key using the `from` field of the `inbox` collection:

```
mongos> sh.shardCollection("social.inbox", {from: 1})
```

 In case our collection already has documents, we should create an index for the shard key field.

The final step is to create a compound index on the `to` and `sent` fields, seeking a better performance on read operations:

```
mongos> db.inbox.createIndex({to: 1, sent: 1})
```

We are now ready to send and read messages in our `inbox` collection. On the `mongos` shell, let's create a message and send it to the recipients:

```
mongos> var msg = {
from: "John",
to: ["Mike", "Billie"],
sent: new Date(),
message: "Hey Mike, Billie"
}; // this command creates a msg variable and stores a message json as a value
mongos> db.inbox.insert(msg); // this command inserts the message on the inbox collection
```

If we want to read Mike's inbox, we should use the following command:

```
mongos> db.inbox.find({to: "Mike"}).sort({sent: -1})
```

The write operation in this design may be considered as efficient. Depending on the number of active users, we will have an even distribution of data across the shards.

On the other hand, viewing an inbox is not so efficient. Every inbox read issues a `find` operation using the `to` field sorted by the `sent` field. Because our collection has the `from` field as a shard key, which means that the messages are grouped by sender on the shards, every query that does not use the shard key will be routed to all shards.

This design applies well if our application is targeted to sending messages. As we need a social application in which you send and read messages, let's take a look at the next design approach, fan out on write.

Fan out on write

With the fan out on write design, we can say that we will have an opposite effect compared to the previous one. While in fan out on read, we reached every shard on the cluster to view an inbox, in fan out on write, we will have the write operations distributed between all the shards.

To implement fan out on write instead of sharding on the sender, we will shard on the recipient of the message. The following command creates the shard key in the `inbox` collection:

```
mongos> sh.shardCollection("social.inbox", {recipient: 1, sent: 1})
```

We will use the same document we used on the fan out on read design. So, to send a message from John to Mike and Billie, we will execute the following commands in the mongos shell:

```
mongos> var msg = {
        "from": "John",
        "to": ["Mike", "Billie"], // recipients
        "sent": new Date(),
        "message": "Hey Mike, Billie"
}
```

```
mongos> for(recipient in msg.to){ // iterate though recipients
msg.recipient = msg.to[recipient]; // creates a recipient field on the
message and stores the recipient of the message
db.inbox.insert(msg); // inserts the msg document for every recipient
}
```

To better understand what is happening, let's do a little code breakdown:

- The first thing that we should do is to create a `msg` variable and store a message in JSON there:

    ```
    var msg = {
            "from": "John",
            "to": ["Mike", "Billie"], // recipients
            "sent": new Date(),
            "message": "Hey Mike, Billie"
    }
    ```

- To send a message to every recipient, we must iterate over the value in the `to` field, create a new field on the message JSON, `msg.recipient`, and store the message's recipient:

```
for(recipient in msg.to){

msg.recipient = msg.to[recipient];
```

- Finally, we insert the message in the `inbox` collection:

```
db.inbox.insert(msg);

}
```

For every recipient of the message, we will insert a new document in the `inbox` collection. The following command, executed on the `mongos` shell, shows Mike's inbox:

```
mongos> db.inbox.find ({recipient: "Mike"}).sort({ sent:-1})

{

    "_id": ObjectId("54fe6319b40b90bd157eb0b8"),

    "from": "John",

    "to": [

        "Mike",

        "Billie"

    ],

    "sent": ISODate("2015-03-10T03:20:03.597Z"),

    "message": "Hey Mike, Billie",

    "recipient": "Mike"

}
```

As the message has both Mike and Billie as recipients, we can also read Billie's inbox:

```
mongos> db.inbox.find ({recipient: "Billie"}).sort({ sent:-1})

{

    "_id": ObjectId("54fe6319b40b90bd157eb0b9"),

    "from": "John",

    "to": [

        "Mike",

        "Billie"

    ],
```

```
    "sent": ISODate("2015-03-10T03:20:03.597Z"),
    "message": "Hey Mike, Billie",
    "recipient": "Billie"
}
```

By doing so, when we are reading a user's inbox, we are targeting a single shard, since we are using the shard key as criteria for the find query.

But, even though we reach only one shard to view an inbox, we will have many random reads when the number of users grows. To deal with this problem, we are going to meet the concept of bucketing.

Fan out on write with buckets

The fan out on write design is a very interesting approach to the social inboxes problem. Every time we need to, we could add more shards to our cluster, and the inboxes data will be evenly distributed between then. However, as we stated before, the random reads we made as our database grows are a bottleneck we must deal with. Although we target a single shard on a read operation by using the shard key as criteria for our find query, we will always have a random read on viewing an inbox. Suppose we have an average of 50 messages by each user, then for each inbox view it will produce 50 random reads. So, when we multiply these random reads by users simultaneously accessing their inboxes, we can imagine how fast we will saturate our database.

In an attempt to reduce this bottleneck, the fan out on write with buckets approach emerges. Fan out with buckets is a refined fan out on write, by bucketing messages together in documents of messages sorted by time.

The implementation of this design is quite different compared to the previous ones. In fan out on write with buckets, we will have two collections:

- One `users` collection
- One `inbox` collection

The `users` collection will have documents with user data. In this document besides the basic user information, we also have a field that stores the total number of inbox messages that the user has.

The `inbox` collection will store documents with a set of user messages. We will have an `owner` field that will identify the user in this collection and a `sequence` field that identifies the bucket. These are the fields that we will shard the `inbox` collection with.

In our example, each bucket will have 50 messages. The following commands will enable sharding on the social database and create the shard key in the `inbox` collection:

```
mongos> sh.enableSharding("social")
mongos> sh.shardCollection("social.inbox", {owner: 1, sequence: 1})
```

As it was previously mentioned, we also have a `users` collection. The following command creates a shard key in the `user` collection:

```
mongos> sh.shardCollection("social.users", {user_name: 1})
```

Now that we have created our shard keys, let's send a message from John to Mike and Billie. The message document will be very similar to the previous one. The difference between them is the `owner` and `sequence` fields. The following code, executed on the `mongos` shell, will send a message from John to Mike and Billie:

```
mongos> var msg = {
    "from": "John",
    "to": ["Mike", "Billie"], //recipients
    "sent": new Date(),
    "message": "Hey Mike, Billie"
}


mongos> for(recipient in msg.to) {

var count = db.users.findAndModify({
            query: {user_name: msg.to[recipient]},
            update:{"$inc":{"msg_count":1}},
            upsert: true,
            new: true}).msg_count;


  var sequence = Math.floor(count/50);

  db.inbox.update({
            owner: msg.to[recipient], sequence: sequence},
            {$push:{"messages":msg}},
            {upsert: true});

}
```

As we did before, to understand to send the message, let's do a code breakdown:

- First, we create a `msg` variable and store message JSON there
- We iterate over the recipients in the `to` field, and execute a `findAndModify` method, where we look for a document in the `users` collection and who the owner of the message recipient is. As we use the `upsert` option with the value `true`, if we did not find the user, then we create a new one. The `update` field has a `$inc` operator, which means that we will increment one to the `msg_count` field. The method also uses a `new` option with the value `true`, and we will have executed the saved document as a result of this command.
- From the returned document, we get the value of the `msg_count` field, which represents the total messages to the user, and store the value on a `count` variable.
- To discover the bucket where the message will be saved, we will use the function `floor` of the `Math` class that is available on the `mongos` shell. As we said before, we will have 50 messages in each bucket, so we will divide the value of the `count` variable by 50, and get the `floor` function of the result. So, for example, if we are sending a third user message, then the bucket to save this message is the result of `Math.floor(3/50)`, which is 0. When we reach the 50th message, the bucket value becomes 1, which means that the next message will be in a new bucket.
- We will update the document in the `inbox` collection that has the `owner` and `sequence` value we calculated. As we use the `upsert` option with the value `true` on the `update` command, it will create the document if it does not exist.

It this way, we will guarantee that a user's inbox is entirely on a single shard. In contrast to fan on write, where we have many random reads when we view a inbox, in fan out on write with buckets, we do one document read for every 50 user messages.

Fan out on write with buckets is without a doubt the best option to a social inbox schema design, when our requirements are to send and read messages efficiently. However, the document size of the `inbox` collection can become a problem. Depending on the messages' sizes, we will have to be careful with our storage.

Summary

Schema design is a better scalability strategy. No matter how many techniques and tools we have at our disposal, to know how our data will be used and dedicate time to our design is the cheaper and long-lasting approach to use.

In the next chapter, you will use everything you've learned until now and create a schema design from scratch for a real-life example.

8
Logging and Real-time Analytics with MongoDB

Throughout this book, many concepts you already knew were presented to you. You have learned how to use them in conjunction with the techniques and tools that MongoDB offers to us. The goal of this chapter is to apply these techniques in a real-life example.

The real-life example we will develop in this chapter explains how to use MongoDB as a persistent storage for a web server's log data—to be more specific, the data from an Nginx web server. By doing this, we will be able to analyze the traffic data of a web application.

We will start this chapter by analyzing the Nginx log format in order to define the information that will be useful for our experiment. After this, we will define the type of analysis we want to perform in MongoDB. Finally, we will design our database schema and implement, by using code, reading and writing data in MongoDB.

For this chapter, we will take into consideration that each host that generates this event consumes this information and sends it to MongoDB. Our focus will not be on the application's architecture or on the code we will produce in our example. So, kind reader, if you do not agree with the code snippets shown here, please, feel free to modify them or create a new one yourself.

That said, this chapter will cover:

- Log data analysis
- What we are looking for
- Designing the schema

Log data analysis

The access log is often ignored by developers, system administrators, or anyone who keeps services on the web. But it is a powerful tool when we need prompt feedback on what is happening for each request on our web server.

The access log keeps information about the server's activities and performance and also tells us about eventual problems. The most common web servers nowadays are Apache HTTPD and Nginx. These web servers have by default two log types: error logs and access logs.

Error logs

As the name suggests, the error log is where the web server will store errors found during the processing of a received request. In general, this type of log is configurable and will write the messages according to the predefined severity level.

Access logs

The access log is where all the received and processed requests are stored. This will be the main object of our study.

The events written in the file are recorded in a predefined layout that can be formatted according to the wishes of those who are managing the server. By default, both Apache HTTPD and Nginx have a format known as **combined**. An example of a log generated in this format is presented as follows:

```
191.32.254.162 - - [29/Mar/2015:16:04:08 -0400] "GET /admin
HTTP/1.1" 200 2529 "-" "Mozilla/5.0 (Macintosh; Intel Mac OS X
10_9_5) AppleWebKit/537.36 (KHTML, like Gecko) Chrome/41.0.2272.104
Safari/537.36"
```

At first sight, it can be a little frightening to see too much information in only one log line. However, if we take a look at the pattern that is being applied in order to generate this log and try to examine it, we will see that it is not so difficult to understand.

The pattern that generates this line on the Nginx web server is presented as follows:

```
$remote_addr - $remote_user [$time_local] "$request" $status $body_bytes_
sent "$http_referer" "$http_user_agent"
```

We will describe each part of this pattern so you get a better understanding:

- $remote_addr: This is the IP address of the client that performed the request on the web server. In our example, this value corresponds to 191.32.254.162.

- $remote_user: This is the authenticated user, if it exists. When an authenticated user is not identified, this field will be filled with a hyphen. In our example, the value is -.

- [$time_local]: This is the time that the request was received on the web server in the format [day/month/year:hour:minute:second zone].

- "$request": This is the client request itself. Also known as a request line. To get a better understanding, we will analyze our request line in the example: "GET /admin HTTP/1.1". First, we have the HTTP verb used by the client. In this case, it was a GET HTTP verb. In the sequence, we have the resource accessed by the client. In this case, the resource accessed was /admin. And last, we have the protocol used by the client. In this case, HTTP/1.1.

- $status: This is the HTTP status code replied to the client by the web server. The possible values for this field are defined in RFC 2616. In our example, the web server returns the status code 200 to the client.

 To learn more about RFC 2616, you can visit http://www.w3.org/Protocols/rfc2616/rfc2616.txt.

- $body_bytes_sent: This is the length in bytes of the response body sent to the client. When you do not have a body, the value will be a hyphen. We must observe that this value does not include the request headers. In our example, the value is 2,529 bytes.

- "$http_referer": This is the contained value in the header "Referer" of the client's request. This value represents where the requested resource is referenced from. When the resource access is performed directly, this field is filled with a hyphen. In our example, the value is -.

- "$http_user_agent": This is the information that the client sends in the User-Agent header. Normally, it is in this header that we can identify the web browser used on the request. In our example, the value for this field is "Mozilla/5.0 (Macintosh; Intel Mac OS X 10_9_5) AppleWebKit/537.36 (KHTML, like Gecko) Chrome/41.0.2272.104 Safari/537.36".

Besides these, we have more variables available to create new log formats. Among these, we highlight:

- `$request_time`: This indicates the total time for the request processing
- `$request_length`: This indicates the total length for the client response, including the headers

Now that we are familiar with the web server access log, we will define what we want to analyze in order to know what the information needs to be logged.

What we are looking for

The information extracted from a web server access log is very rich and give us good material for infinite possibilities of study. Being simple and direct, it is possible to count the number of requests that our web server receives just by counting the number of lines that the access log has. But we can expand our analysis and try to measure the average of the data traffic in bytes over the time, for example.

Recently, one of the most widely used services is the application performance management system, also known as **APMs**. Nowadays, these services are commonly offered as software-as-a-service and the main goal is to give us a view of an application's performance and health.

APMs are a good example of what can be analyzed based on the information extracted from the access log, due to the fact that a good part of the information that APMs generate is based on the access logs.

Attention! I am not saying that an APM works based only on the access log, but a good part of the information generated by APMs can be extracted from the access log. Okay?

To learn more, visit `https://en.wikipedia.org/wiki/Application_performance_management`.

As said at the beginning of this chapter, we do not have any intention of coding or creating an entire system, but we will show in practice how we can keep the access log information for an eventual analysis using MongoDB.

Based on APMs, we will structure our example on an analysis of web server resource throughput. It is possible to perform this analysis only with the information contained on the web server access log. To do so, what data do we need in our access log? And should we use the combined format?

Measuring the traffic on the web server

The throughput in our web server will be estimated based on the number of requests for a given period of time, that is, requests in a day, in an hour, in a minute, or in a second. The number of requests per minute is a very reasonable measure for a real-time monitoring.

The throughput is calculated by counting the requests processed in our web server. Because of this, it is not necessary to work with specific data from the access log. Nevertheless, in order to make possible a richer further analysis of our data, we will create a specific log format that will collect request information such as the HTTP status code, the request time, and length.

Both Apache HTTP and Nginx allow us to customize the access log or to create a new file with a custom format. The second option seems to be perfect. Before we start to configure our web server, we will create our log format using the variables previously explained. Just remember that we are working on an Nginx web server.

```
$remote_addr [$time_local] "$request" $status $request_time $request_length
```

As we defined our log format, we can configure our Nginx web server. To do so, let's perform the following steps:

1. First of all, to define this new format in Nginx, we need to edit the `nginx.conf` file, adding a new entry in the HTTP element with the new log format:

   ```
   log_format custom_format '$remote_addr [$time_local] "$request" $status $request_time $request_length';
   ```

2. Now we need to add another entry in `nginx.conf` file that defines in which file the new custom log will be written:

   ```
   access_log /var/log/nginx/custom_access.log custom_format;
   ```

3. To apply our changes, reload the Nginx web server executing the following command in a terminal:

   /usr/sbin/nginx reload

4. After reloading the Nginx server, we can look at our new log file, `/var/log/nginx/custom_access.log`, and check whether the lines are like the following lines:

   ```
   191.32.254.162 [29/Mar/2015:18:35:26 -0400] "GET / HTTP/1.1" 200 0.755 802
   ```

Log format configured, web server set up; it is time to design our schema.

Designing the schema

Something that has been repeated several times during this book is the importance of knowing our data and what it will be used for. And now, more than ever, in this practical exercise we will design our schema step by step, considering every detail involved in this.

In the previous section, we defined the data set that we want to extract from the web server access logs. The next step is to list the requirements that are associated with the clients of the database. As said previously, one process will be responsible for capturing the information from the log files and writing them in MongoDB, and another process will read the information already persisted in the database.

A point of concern is the performance during the document writing in MongoDB because it is important to ensure that the information will be generated almost in realtime. Since we do not have a previous estimation of the data volume per second, we will be optimistic. Let's consider that we will have a huge volume of data all the time coming from the web server to our MongoDB instance.

Taking into account this requirement, we will be worried about the data dimensions that will increase over time. More events imply that more documents will be inserted. These are the main requirements for our system to operate well.

At first sight, we can imagine that it is all about defining the document format and persisting it into a collection. But thinking in this way is to ignore the well-known MongoDB schema flexibility. So we will analyze the problem of throughput in order to define where and how to persist the information.

Capturing an event request

The web server throughput analysis is maybe the simplest task. In a simple way, the measure of the number of events will give us a number that represents the web server's throughput.

So, if for each generated event a write document is performed stating the time of this operation, does it mean that we can easily get the throughput? Yes! Thus, the easiest way to represent a MongoDB document where we can analyze the throughput is the following:

```
{

    "_id" : ObjectId("5518ce5c322fa17f4243f85f"),
```

```
    "request_line" : "191.32.254.162 [29/Mar/2015:18:35:26 -0400] \"GET /
media/catalog/product/image/2.jpg HTTP/1.1\" 200 0.000 867"

}
```

When executing the `count` method in the document collection, we will get the web server's throughput value. Assuming that we have a collection called `events`, in order to find out the throughput, we must execute the following command in the mongod shell:

`db.events.find({}).count()`

This command returns the total of generated events until now on our web server. But, is this the number that we want? No. There is no point in having the total number of events without placing it in a given period of time. Would it be of any use to have 10,000 events processed by the web server until now without knowing when we started recording these events or even when the last event was generated?

If we want to count the events in a given period of time, the easiest way to do so is by including a field that will represent the event's creation date. An example for this document is shown as follows:

```
{

    "_id" : ObjectId("5518ce5c322fa17f4243f85f"),

    "request_line" : "191.32.254.162 [29/Mar/2015:18:35:26 -0400] \"GET /
media/catalog/product/image/2.jpg HTTP/1.1\" 0.000 867",

    "date_created" : ISODate("2015-03-30T04:17:32.246Z")

}
```

As a result, we can check the total number of requests in the web server in a given period of time by executing a query. The simplest way to perform this query is to use the aggregation framework. The execution of the following command on the mongod shell will return the total of requests per minute:

```
db.events.aggregate(
{
    $group: {
        _id: {
            request_time: {
```

```
                month: {
                    $month: "$date_created"
                },
                day: {
                    $dayOfMonth: "$date_created"
                },
                year: {
                    $year: "$date_created"
                },
                hour: {
                    $hour: "$date_created"
                },
                min: {
                    $minute: "$date_created"
                }
            }
        },
        count: {
            $sum: 1
        }
    }
})
```

> The aggregation pipeline has its limits. If the command result returns a single document that exceeds the BSON document size, an error is produced. Since MongoDB's 2.6 release, the `aggregate` command returns a cursor, so it can return result sets of any size.
>
> You can find more about aggregation pipeline limits in the MongoDB reference manual at `http://docs.mongodb.org/manual/core/aggregation-pipeline-limits/`.

In the command pipeline, we defined the `$group` stage to group the documents per day, month, year, hour, and minute. And we count everything using the `$sum` operator. From this `aggregate` command's execution, we will have, as an example, documents such as these:

```
{
    "_id": {
        "request_time": {
```

```
                "month": 3,
                "day": 30,
                "year": 2015,
                "hour": 4,
                "min": 48
            }
        },
        "count": 50
    }
    {
        "_id": {
            "request_time": {
                "month": 3,
                "day": 30,
                "year": 2015,
                "hour": 4,
                "min": 38
            }
        },
        "count": 13
    }
    {
        "_id": {
            "request_time": {
                "month": 3,
                "day": 30,
                "year": 2015,
                "hour": 4,
                "min": 17
            }
        },
        "count": 26
    }
```

In this output, it is possible to know how many requests the web server received in a certain time period. This happens due to the `$group` operator behavior, which takes documents that match a query and then collects groups of documents based on one or more fields. We took each part of our `$date_created` field, such as the month, day, year, hour, and minute, to the group stage of the aggregation pipeline.

If you want to know which resource is accessed the most often in your web server with the higher throughput, none of these options fit this request. However, a fast solution for this problem is easily reachable. At first sight, the fastest way is to deconstruct the event and create a more complex document, as you can see in the following example:

```
{
    "_id" : ObjectId("5519baca82d8285709606ce9"),
    "remote_address" : "191.32.254.162",
    "date_created" : ISODate("2015-03-29T18:35:25Z"),
    "http_method" : "GET",
    "resource" : "/media/catalog/product/cache/1/image/200x267/9df78eab33
525d08d6e5fb8d27136e95/2/_/2.jpg",
    "http_version" : "HTTP/1.1",
    "status": 200,
    "request_time" : 0,
    "request_length" : 867
}
```

By using this document design, it is possible to know the resource throughput per minute with the help of an aggregation framework:

```
db.events.aggregate([
    {
        $group: {
            _id: "$resource",
            hits: {
                $sum: 1
            }
        }
    },
    {
```

```
        $project: {
            _id: 0,
            resource: "$_id",
            throughput: {
                $divide: [
                    "$hits",
                    1440
                ]
            }
        }
    },
    {

        $sort: {
            throughput: -1
        }
    }
])
```

In the preceding pipeline, the first step is to group by resource and to count how many times a request on the resource occurred during an entire day. The next step is to use the operator $project and, together with the operator $divide, use the number of hits in a given resource and calculate the average per minute by dividing by 1,440 minutes, that is, the total of minutes in a day or 24 hours. Finally, we order the results in descending order to view which resources have the higher throughput.

To keep things clear, we will execute the pipeline step by step and explain the results for each step. In the execution of the first phase, we have the following:

```
db.events.aggregate([{$group: {_id: "$resource", hits: {$sum: 1}}}])
```

This execution groups the event collection documents by field resource and counts the number of occurrences of field hits when we use the operator $sum with the value 1. The returned result is demonstrated as follows:

```
{ "_id" : "/", "hits" : 5201 }
{ "_id" : "/legal/faq", "hits" : 1332 }
{ "_id" : "/legal/terms", "hits" : 3512 }
```

In the second phase of the pipeline, we use the operator `$project`, which will give us the value of hits per minute:

```
db.documents.aggregate([
    {
        $group: {
            _id: "$resource",
            hits: {
                $sum: 1
            }
        }
    },
    {
        $project: {
            _id: 0,
            resource: "$_id",
            throughput: {
                $divide: [
                    "$hits",
                    1440
                ]
            }
        }
    }
])
```

The following is the result of this phase:

```
{ "resource" : "/", "throughput" : 3.6118055555555557 }
{ "resource" : "/legal/faq", "throughput" : 0.925 }
{ "resource" : "/legal/terms", "throughput" : 2.438888888888889 }
```

The last phase of the pipeline is to order the results by throughput in descending order:

```
db.documents.aggregate([
    {
        $group: {
```

```
            _id: "$resource",
            hits: {
                $sum: 1
            }
        }
    },
    {

        $project: {
            _id: 0,
            resource: "$_id",
            throughput: {
                $divide: [
                    "$hits",
                    1440
                ]
            }
        }
    },
    {

        $sort: {
            throughput: -1
        }
    }
])
```

The output produced is like the following:

```
{ "resource" : "/", "throughput" : 3.6118055555555557 }
{ "resource" : "/legal/terms", "throughput" : 2.438888888888889 }
{ "resource" : "/legal/faq", "throughput" : 0.925 }
```

It looks like we succeeded in obtaining a good design for our document.
Now we can extract the desired analysis and other analyses, as we will see further, and for that reason we can stop for now. Wrong! We will review our requirements, compare them to the model that we designed, and try to figure out whether it was the best solution.

Our desire is to know the measure of throughput per minute for all web server resources. In the model we designed, one document is created per event in our web server, and by using the aggregation framework we can calculate the information that we need for our analysis.

What can be wrong in this solution? Well, if you think it's the number of documents in the collection, you are right. One document per event can generate huge collections depending on the web server traffic. Obviously, we can adopt the strategy of using shards, and distribute the collection through many hosts. But first, we will see how we can take advantage of the schema flexibility in MongoDB in order to reduce the collection size and optimize the queries.

A one-document solution

Having one document per event may be advantageous if we consider that we will have a huge amount of information to create an analysis. But in the example that we are trying to solve, it is expensive to persist one document for each HTTP request.

We will take advantage of the schema flexibility in MongoDB that will help us to grow documents over time. The following proposal has the main goal of reducing the number of persisted documents, also optimizing the queries for read and write operations in our collection.

The document we are looking for should be able to provide us all the information needed in order to know the resource throughput in requests per minute; thus we can have a document with this structure:

- A field with the resource
- A field with the event date
- A field with the minute that the event happened, and the total hits

The following document implements all the requirements described in the preceding list:

```
{
    "_id" : ObjectId("552005f5e2202a2f6001d7b0"),
    "resource" : "/",
    "date" : ISODate("2015-05-02T03:00:00Z"),
    "daily" : 215840,
```

```
"minute" : {
    "0" : 90,

    "1" : 150,
    "2" : 143,
    ...
    "1349": 210
  }
}
```

With this document design, we can retrieve the number of events happening in a certain resource every minute. We can also know, by the daily field, the total requests during the day and use this to calculate whatever we want, such as requests per minute, or requests per hour, for instance.

To demonstrate the write and read operations we could make on this collection, we will make use of JavaScript code running on the Node.js platform. So, before continuing, we must make sure we have Node.js installed on our machine.

 If you need help, you will find more information at `http://nodejs.org`.

The firs thing we should do is to create a directory where our application will live. In a terminal, execute the following command:

`mkdir throughput_project`

Next we navigate to the directory we created and initiate the project:

`cd throughput_project`

`npm init`

Answer all the questions asked by the wizard to create the initial structure of our new project. At the moment, we will have a `package.json` file based on the answers we gave.

The next step is to set up the MongoDB driver for our project. We can do this by editing the `package.json` file, including the driver reference for its dependencies, or by executing the following command:

`npm install mongodb --save`

The preceding command will install the MongoDB driver for our project and save the reference in the `package.json` file. Our file should look like this:

```
{
  "name": "throughput_project",
  "version": "1.0.0",
  "description": "",
  "main": "app.js",
  "scripts": {
    "test": "echo \"Error: no test specified\" && exit 1"
  },
  "author": "Wilson da Rocha França",
  "license": "ISC",
  "dependencies": {
    "mongodb": "^2.0.25"
  }
}
```

The last step is to create the `app.js` file with our sample code. The following is sample code that shows us how to count an event on our web server and record it in our collection:

```
var fs = require('fs');
var util = require('util');
var mongo = require('mongodb').MongoClient;
var assert = require('assert');


// Connection URL
var url = 'mongodb://127.0.0.1:27017/monitoring;
// Create the date object and set hours, minutes,
// seconds and milliseconds to 00:00:00.000
var today = new Date();
today.setHours(0, 0, 0, 0);


var logDailyHit = function(db, resource, callback){
  // Get the events collection
  var collection = db.collection('events');
  // Update daily stats
  collection.update({resource: resource, date: today},
    {$inc : {daily: 1}}, {upsert: true},
    function(error, result){
      assert.equal(error, null);
      assert.equal(1, result.result.n);
```

```
        console.log("Daily Hit logged");
        callback(result);
    });
}


var logMinuteHit = function(db, resource, callback) {
    // Get the events collection
    var collection = db.collection('events');
    // Get current minute to update
    var currentDate = new Date();
    var minute = currentDate.getMinutes();
    var hour = currentDate.getHours();
    // We calculate the minute of the day
    var minuteOfDay = minute + (hour * 60);
    var minuteField = util.format('minute.%s', minuteOfDay);
    // Create a update object
    var update = {};
    var inc = {};
    inc[minuteField] = 1;
    update['$inc'] = inc;


    // Update minute stats
    collection.update({resource: resource, date: today},
        update, {upsert: true}, function(error, result){
            assert.equal(error, null);
            assert.equal(1, result.result.n);
            console.log("Minute Hit logged");
            callback(result);
    });
}


// Connect to MongoDB and log
mongo.connect(url, function(err, db) {
    assert.equal(null, err);
    console.log("Connected to server");
    var resource = "/";
    logDailyHit(db, resource, function() {
        logMinuteHit(db, resource, function(){
            db.close();
            console.log("Disconnected from server")
        });
    });
});
```

The preceding sample code is quite simple. In it, we have the `logDailyHit` function, which is responsible for logging an event and incrementing one unit in the document `daily` field. The second function is the `logMinuteHit` function, which is responsible for logging the occurrence of an event and incrementing the document `minute` field that represents the current minute in the day. Both functions have an update query that has an `upsert` option with the value `true` if the document does not exist, in which case it will be created.

When we execute the following command, we will record an event on the resource `"/"`. To run the code, just navigate to the project directory and execute the following command:

```
node app.js
```

If everything is fine, we should see the following output after running the command:

```
Connected to server
Daily Hit logged
Minute Hit logged
Disconnected from server
```

To get a feel for this, we will execute a `findOne` command on the mongod shell and watch the result:

```
db.events.findOne()
{
    "_id" : ObjectId("5520ade00175e1fb3361b860"),
    "resource" : "/",
    "date" : ISODate("2015-04-04T03:00:00Z"),
    "daily" : 383,
    "minute" : {
        "0" : 90,
        "1" : 150,
        "2" : 143
    }
}
```

In addition to everything that the previous models can give us, this one has some advantages over them. The first thing we notice is that, every time we register a new event happening on the web server, we will manipulate only one document. The next advantage also lies in how easy we can find the information we are looking for, given a specific resource, since we have the information for an entire day in one document, which will lead to us to manipulating fewer documents in each query.

The way this schema design deals with time will give us many benefits when we think about reports. Both textual and graphical representations can be easily extracted from this collection for historical or real-time analysis.

However, as well as the previous approaches, we will have to deal with a few limitations too. As we have seen, we increment both the `daily` field and a `minute` field in an event document as they occur on the web server. When no event in a resource was reported for that day, then a new document will be created since we are using the `upsert` option on the update query. The same thing will happen if an event occurs in a resource for the first time in a given minute—the `$inc` operator will create the new `minute` field and set `"1"` as the value. This means that our document will grow over time, and will exceed the size MongoDB allocated initially for it. MongoDB automatically performs a reallocation operation every time the space allocated to the document is full. This reallocation operation that happens through the entire day has a direct impact on the database's performance.

What we should do? Live with it? No. We could reduce the impact of a reallocation operation by adding a process that preallocates space for our document. In summary, we will give the application the responsibility for creating a document with all the minutes we can have in a day, and initializing every field with the value 0. By doing this, we will avoid too many reallocation operations by MongoDB during the day.

 To learn more about record allocation strategies, visit the MongoDB reference user manual at `http://docs.mongodb.org/manual/core/storage/#record-allocation-strategies`.

To give an example of how we can preallocate the document space, we can create a new function in our app.js file:

```
var fs = require('fs');
var util = require('util');
var mongo = require('mongodb').MongoClient;
var assert = require('assert');


// Connection URL
var url = 'mongodb://127.0.0.1:27017/monitoring';


var preAllocate = function(db, resource, callback){
  // Get the events collection
  var collection = db.collection('events');
  var now = new Date();
  now.setHours(0,0,0,0);
  // Create the minute document
  var minuteDoc = {};
  for(i = 0; i < 1440; i++){
    minuteDoc[i] = 0;
  }
  // Update minute stats
  collection.update(
      {resource: resource,
        date: now,
        daily: 0},
      {$set: {minute: minuteDoc}},
      {upsert: true}, function(error, result){
        assert.equal(error, null);
        assert.equal(1, result.result.n);
        console.log("Pre-allocated successfully!");
        callback(result);
    });
}
```

```
// Connect to MongoDB and log
mongo.connect(url, function(err, db) {
  assert.equal(null, err);
  console.log("Connected to server");
  var resource = "/";
  preAllocate(db, resource, function(){
    db.close();
    console.log("Disconnected from server")
  });
});
```

Downloading the example code

You can download the example code files from your account at `http://www.packtpub.com` for all the Packt Publishing books you have purchased. If you purchased this book elsewhere, you can visit `http://www.packtpub.com/support` and register to have the files e-mailed directly to you.

To preallocate space in the current date to the `"/"` resource, just run the following command:

```
node app.js
```

The output of the execution is something like this:

```
Connected to server
Pre-allocated successfully!
Disconnected from server
```

We can run a `findOne` command on the mongod shell to check the new document. The document created is very long, so we will show just a piece of it:

```
db.events.findOne();
{
    "_id" : ObjectId("551fd893eb6efdc4e71260a0"),
    "daily" : 0,
    "date" : ISODate("2015-04-06T03:00:00Z"),
    "resource" : "/",
    "minute" : {
```

```
        "0" : 0,
        "1" : 0,
        "2" : 0,
        "3" : 0,
        ...
        "1439" : 0,
    }
}
```

It is recommended that we preallocate the document before midnight to ensure smooth functioning of the application. If we schedule this creation with an appropriate safety margin, we are not running any risk of creating the document for an event occurrence after midnight.

Well, with the reallocation problem solved, we can go back to the issue that initiated our document redesign: the growth of our data.

Even reducing the number of documents in our collection to one document per event per day, we can still run into a problem with storage space. This can happen when we have too many resources receiving events on our web server, and we cannot predict how many new resources we will have in our application's lifecycle. In order to solve this issue, we will use two different techniques: TTL indexes and sharding.

TTL indexes

It is not always the case that we need to have all log information stored on our servers forever. It has become a standard practice by operations people to limit the number of files stored on disk.

By the same reasoning, we can limit the number of documents we need living in our collection. To make this happen, we could create a TTL index on the date field, specifying how long one document will exist in the collection. Just remember that, once we create a TTL index, MongoDB will automatically remove the expired documents from the collection.

Suppose that the event hit information is useful just during one year. We will create an index on the date field with the property expireAfterSeconds with 31556926 as the value, which corresponds to one year in seconds.

The following command, executed on the mongod shell, creates the index on our events collection:

```
db.monitoring.createIndex({date: 1}, {expireAfterSeconds: 31556926})
```

If the index does not exist, the output should look like this:

```
{
    "createdCollectionAutomatically" : false,
    "numIndexesBefore" : 1,
    "numIndexesAfter" : 2,
    "ok" : 1
}
```

Once this is done, our documents will live in our collection for one year, based on the date field, and after this MongoDB will remove them automatically.

Sharding

If you are one of those people who have infinite resources and would like to have a lot of information stored on disk, then one solution to mitigate the storage space problem is to distribute the data by sharding your collection.

And, as we stated before, we should increase our efforts when we choose the shard key, since it is through the shard key that we will guarantee that our read and write operations will be equally distributed by the shards, that is, one query will target a single shard or a few shards on the cluster.

Once we have full control over how many resources (or pages) we have on our web server and how this number will grow or decrease, the resource name becomes a good choice for a shard key. However, if we have a resource that has more requests (or events) than others, then we will have a shard that will be overloaded. To avoid this, we will include the date field to compose the shard key, which will also give us better performance on query executions that include this field in the criteria.

Remember: our goal is not to explain the setup of a sharded cluster. We will present to you the command that shards our collection, taking into account that you previously created your sharded cluster.

To shard the events collection with the shard key we choose, we will execute the following command on the mongos shell:

```
mongos> sh.shardCollection("monitoring.events", {resource: 1, date: 1})
```

The expected output is:

```
{ "collectionsharded" : "monitoring.events", "ok" : 1 }
```

 If our events collection has any document in it, we will need to create an index where the shard key is a prefix before sharding the collection. To create the index, execute the following command:

```
db.monitoring.createIndex({resource: 1, date: 1})
```

With the collection with the shard enabled, we will have more capacity to store data in the events collection, and a potential gain in performance as the data grows.

Now that we've designed our document and prepared our collection to receive a huge amount of data, let's perform some queries!

Querying for reports

Until now, we have focused our efforts on storing the data in our database. This does not mean that we are not concerned about read operations. Everything we did was made possible by outlining the profile of our application, and trying to cover all the requirements to prepare our database for whatever comes our way.

So, we will now illustrate some of the possibilities that we have to query our collection, in order to build reports based on the stored data.

If what we need is real-time information about the total hits on a resource, we can use our daily field to query the data. With this field, we can determine the total hits on a resource at a particular time of day, or even the average requests per minute on the resource based on the minute of the day.

To query the total hits based on the current time of the day, we will create a new function called getCurrentDayhits and, to query the average request per minute in a day, we will create the getCurrentMinuteStats function in the app.js file:

```
var fs = require('fs');
var util = require('util');
var mongo = require('mongodb').MongoClient;
var assert = require('assert');

// Connection URL
var url = 'mongodb://127.0.0.1:27017/monitoring';
```

```javascript
var getCurrentDayhitStats = function(db, resource, callback){
  // Get the events collection
  var collection = db.collection('events');
  var now = new Date();
  now.setHours(0,0,0,0);
  collection.findOne({resource: "/", date: now},
    {daily: 1}, function(err, doc) {
    assert.equal(err, null);
    console.log("Document found.");
    console.dir(doc);
    callback(doc);
  });
}


var getCurrentMinuteStats = function(db, resource, callback){
  // Get the events collection
  var collection = db.collection('events');
  var now = new Date();
  // get hours and minutes and hold
  var hour = now.getHours()
  var minute = now.getMinutes();
  // calculate minute of the day to create field name
  var minuteOfDay = minute + (hour * 60);
  var minuteField = util.format('minute.%s', minuteOfDay);
  // set hour to zero to put on criteria
  now.setHours(0, 0, 0, 0);
  // create the project object and set minute of the day value
  var project = {};
  project[minuteField] = 1;
  collection.findOne({resource: "/", date: now},
    project, function(err, doc) {
    assert.equal(err, null);
    console.log("Document found.");
    console.dir(doc);
    callback(doc);
  });
}


// Connect to MongoDB and log
mongo.connect(url, function(err, db) {
  assert.equal(null, err);
```

```
      console.log("Connected to server");
      var resource = "/";
      getCurrentDayhitStats(db, resource, function(){
        getCurrentMinuteStats(db, resource, function(){
          db.close();
          console.log("Disconnected from server");
        });
      });
    });
```

To see the magic happening, we should run the following command in the terminal:

`node app.js`

If everything is fine, the output should look like this:

```
Connected to server
Document found.
{ _id: 551fdacdeb6efdc4e71260a2, daily: 27450 }
Document found.
{ _id: 551fdacdeb6efdc4e71260a2, minute: { '183': 142 } }
Disconnected from server
```

Another possibility is to retrieve daily information to calculate the average requests per minute of a resource, or to get the set of data between two dates to build a graph or a table.

The following code has two new functions, `getAverageRequestPerMinuteStats`, which calculates the average number of requests per minute of a resource, and `getBetweenDatesDailyStats`, which shows how to retrieve the set of data between two dates. Let's see what the `app.js` file looks like:

```
var fs = require('fs');
var util = require('util');
var mongo = require('mongodb').MongoClient;
var assert = require('assert');

// Connection URL
var url = 'mongodb://127.0.0.1:27017/monitoring';

var getAverageRequestPerMinuteStats = function(db, resource,
callback){
  // Get the events collection
```

```
var collection = db.collection('events');
var now = new Date();
// get hours and minutes and hold
var hour = now.getHours()
var minute = now.getMinutes();
// calculate minute of the day to get the avg
var minuteOfDay = minute + (hour * 60);
// set hour to zero to put on criteria
now.setHours(0, 0, 0, 0);
// create the project object and set minute of the day value
collection.findOne({resource: resource, date: now},
  {daily: 1}, function(err, doc) {
  assert.equal(err, null);
  console.log("The avg rpm is: "+doc.daily / minuteOfDay);
  console.dir(doc);
  callback(doc);
  });
}

var getBetweenDatesDailyStats = function(db, resource, dtFrom,
dtTo, callback){
  // Get the events collection
  var collection = db.collection('events');
  // set hours for date parameters
  dtFrom.setHours(0,0,0,0);
  dtTo.setHours(0,0,0,0);
  collection.find({date:{$gte: dtFrom, $lte: dtTo}, resource:
  resource},
  {date: 1, daily: 1},{sort: [['date',
  1]]}).toArray(function(err, docs) {
    assert.equal(err, null);
    console.log("Documents founded.");
    console.dir(docs);
    callback(docs);
  });
}


// Connect to MongoDB and log
mongo.connect(url, function(err, db) {
  assert.equal(null, err);
  console.log("Connected to server");
  var resource = "/";
```

```
getAverageRequestPerMinuteStats(db, resource, function(){
  var now = new Date();
  var yesterday = new Date(now.getTime());
  yesterday.setDate(now.getDate() -1);
  getBetweenDatesDailyStats(db, resource, yesterday, now,
  function(){
    db.close();
    console.log("Disconnected from server");
  });

});
});
```

As you can see, there are many ways to query the data in the events collection. These were some very simple examples of how to extract the data, but they were functional and reliable ones.

Summary

This chapter showed you an example of the process of designing a schema from scratch, in order to solve a real-life problem. We began with a detailed problem and its requirements and evolved the schema design to have better use of available resources. The sample code based on the problem is very simple, but will serve as a basis for your life-long learning. Great!

In this last chapter, we had the opportunity to make, in just a few pages, a journey back to the first chapters of this book and apply the concepts that were introduced along the way. But, as you must have realized by now, MongoDB is a young, full of database that is full of possibilities. Its adoption by the community around it—and that includes your own—gets bigger with each new release. Thus, if you find yourself faced with a new challenge that you realize that has more than one single solution, carry out any test deem necessary or useful. Colleagues can also help, so talk to them. And always keep in mind that a good design is the one that fits your needs.

Index

Symbols

T

tag sets 109
time to live (TTL) function 123
traffic
  measuring, on web server 149
TTL function
  using 124
TTL index 83, 84

U

unique indexes 85

W

web server
  traffic, measuring on 149
wide-column stores 5
write concerns 63

write operations
  $inc operator 62
  $rename operator 62
  $set operator 61
  $unset operator 62
  bulk write operations, performing 68, 69
  defining 58
  insert interface 59
  update interface 60
  write concern 63

Thank you for buying
MongoDB Data Modeling

About Packt Publishing

Packt, pronounced 'packed', published its first book, *Mastering phpMyAdmin for Effective MySQL Management*, in April 2004, and subsequently continued to specialize in publishing highly focused books on specific technologies and solutions.

Our books and publications share the experiences of your fellow IT professionals in adapting and customizing today's systems, applications, and frameworks. Our solution-based books give you the knowledge and power to customize the software and technologies you're using to get the job done. Packt books are more specific and less general than the IT books you have seen in the past. Our unique business model allows us to bring you more focused information, giving you more of what you need to know, and less of what you don't.

Packt is a modern yet unique publishing company that focuses on producing quality, cutting-edge books for communities of developers, administrators, and newbies alike. For more information, please visit our website at www.packtpub.com.

About Packt Open Source

In 2010, Packt launched two new brands, Packt Open Source and Packt Enterprise, in order to continue its focus on specialization. This book is part of the Packt Open Source brand, home to books published on software built around open source licenses, and offering information to anybody from advanced developers to budding web designers. The Open Source brand also runs Packt's Open Source Royalty Scheme, by which Packt gives a royalty to each open source project about whose software a book is sold.

Writing for Packt

We welcome all inquiries from people who are interested in authoring. Book proposals should be sent to author@packtpub.com. If your book idea is still at an early stage and you would like to discuss it first before writing a formal book proposal, then please contact us; one of our commissioning editors will get in touch with you.

We're not just looking for published authors; if you have strong technical skills but no writing experience, our experienced editors can help you develop a writing career, or simply get some additional reward for your expertise.

Learning MongoDB

ISBN: 978-1-78398-392-6   Duration: 3:26 mins

A comprehensive guide to using MongoDB for ultra-fast, fault tolerant management of big data, including advanced data analysis

1. Master MapReduce and the MongoDB aggregation framework for sophisticated manipulation of large sets of data.

2. Manage databases and collections, including backup, recovery, and security.

3. Discover how to secure your data using SSL, both from the client and via programming languages.

MongoDB Cookbook

ISBN: 978-1-78216-194-3   Paperback: 388 pages

Over 80 practical recipes to design, deploy, and administer MongoDB

1. Gain a thorough understanding of some of the key features of MongoDB.

2. Learn the techniques necessary to solve frequent MongoDB problems.

3. Packed full of step-by-step recipes to help you with installation, design, and deployment.

Please check **www.PacktPub.com** for information on our titles

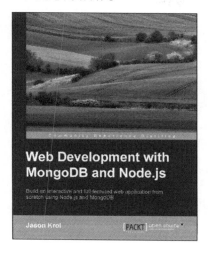

Web Development with MongoDB and Node.js

ISBN: 978-1-78398-730-6   Paperback: 294 pages

Build an interactive and full-featured web application from scratch using Node.js and MongoDB

1. Configure your development environment to use Node.js and MongoDB.

2. Explore the power of development using JavaScript in the full stack of a web application.

3. A practical guide with clear instructions to design and develop a complete web application from start to finish.

Pentaho Analytics for MongoDB

ISBN: 978-1-78216-835-5   Paperback: 146 pages

Combine Pentaho Analytics and MongoDB to create powerful analysis and reporting solutions

1. This is a step-by-step guide that will have you quickly creating eye-catching data visualizations.

2. Includes a sample MongoDB database of web clickstream events for learning how to model and query MongoDB data.

3. Full of tips, images, and exercises that cover the Pentaho development lifecycle.

Please check **www.PacktPub.com** for information on our titles

Made in the USA
San Bernardino, CA
29 August 2016